Third Edition

Q solutions

Quality and Performance Improvement

Third Edition

Q Solutions: Essential Resources for the Healthcare Quality Professional

Quality and Performance Improvement

Susan V. White, PhD RN CPHQ NEA-BC FNAHQ

Series Editors

Luc R. Pelletier, MSN PMHCNS-BC CPHQ FNAHQ FAAN
Christy L. Beaudin, PhD LCSW CPHQ FNAHQ

NAHQ
National Association for Healthcare Quality
Chicago, IL

Other titles in the *Q Solutions* Suite

Leadership and Management
Healthcare Safety
Information Management
Regulation, Accreditation, and Continuous Readiness

 First edition published in 2005. Second edition published in 2008.
ISBN 978-0-9858336-1-9

National Association for Healthcare Quality
8735 W. Higgins Road, Suite 300
Chicago, IL 60631
www.nahq.org

For the National Association for Healthcare Quality
Stacy Sochacki, Executive Director
Beth Zemach, Senior Programs and Product Analyst
Karen Schrimmer, Practice Content Manager
June Pinyo, MA, Managing Editor
Monica Piotrowski, Associate Editor
Sonya Jones, Senior Graphic Designer

Printed in the United States of America
Third Edition

Contents

Tables

Figures

Foreword to the Third Edition

Healthcare is at a transformative and exciting time as we embark on new models of delivering care. Prominent focal points during this essential time are quality, safety, innovation, and the technology needed to bring higher levels of performance with lower costs. During 2011 and 2012, the National Association for Healthcare Quality (NAHQ) has been preparing for the transition by reenergizing our purpose and vision and solidifying our strategies for meaningful work that benefits our stakeholders. Our challenge is determining how to provide the greatest value to our members, certificants, and consumers of NAHQ products while continuing to expand our reach.

We believe it to be of primary importance to coordinate the work of the NAHQ Board of Directors, staff, and teams, as well as the Healthcare Quality Certification Commission (HQCC) to ensure NAHQ products are ready for the market previous to when programs are offered. A prime example of the effort is the third edition of *Q Solutions*.

I take this opportunity to personally thank Luc R. Pelletier, MSN PMHCNS-BC CPHQ FNAHQ FAAN, and Christy L. Beaudin, PhD LCSW CPHQ FNAHQ, for leading this major revision to *Q Solutions* with the most current information available. By providing continuity, intellectual capital, and fortitude to this important NAHQ goal, we have the product ready to deliver to you. The NAHQ Board called on a number of key people throughout the country to support the writing and review of the content, which coordinates with the Certified Professional in Healthcare Quality (CPHQ) content outline's main divisions. I thank each of them and the NAHQ staff for helping to bring this valuable resource to market.

This edition of *Q Solutions* features a new approach to presentating content. By placing the information within individual modules, purchasers may obtain a module specific to his or her needs. The availability of the first four modules (and fifth module soon after) of the third edition coincides with updates to the United States regulation and accreditation content HQCC will begin using in January of 2013. I am certain all of you will want to share this updated resource with your colleagues in the field of healthcare quality. These resources will motivate you to excel even further.

My career development and leadership style have been enriched by many individuals, especially those who have brought their best into this wonderful organization. NAHQ constituents are my network for identifying, learning about, and understanding changes that are happening rapidly and continuously within care delivery. They enhance their workplaces, and patients benefit from their commitment to achieving healthcare improvement. Promoting safe, effective, and efficient practices through education, certification, and advocacy are key components. I encourage each of you to identify the strengths in the people and the products of NAHQ. Enjoy the third edition of *Q Solutions*.

Betty Brown, MBA MSN RN CPHQ FNAHQ
NAHQ President, 2011–2012

Preface

Healthcare is complex and at times confusing to customers. Delivery systems, health plans, solo and group practitioners, employers, and government agencies seek ways to achieve the Triple Aim—ensure quality of care for the individual, improve the health of the population, and control costs. Developing, deploying, and sustaining appropriate quality strategies pose challenges and opportunities for healthcare quality professionals. Thoughtful strategies employ effective, efficient, and evidence-based approaches to measure, monitor, and determine outcomes. Did the actions and interventions yield intended goals and objectives for improved quality and performance excellence? The healthcare quality professional must successfully navigate the system to demonstrate quality and safety. The application of sound theoretical and methodological practices is imperative. *Q Solutions* covers the breadth and depth of critical areas for professional development and leadership, including frameworks for quality management, the linking of science with practice, and the translation of data into practical information that can be used and understood by any customer, whether it is a practitioner, third-party payer, or consumer.

The development of the third edition of *Q Solutions* was informed by the most recent Healthcare Quality Certification Commission's (HQCC's) practice analysis. The practice analysis assesses the current functions and competencies for certified professionals in healthcare quality. Organized under the HQCC detailed content outline, the following modules were created:

- *Leadership and Management*
- *Quality and Performance Improvement*
- *Healthcare Safety*
- *Information Management*
- *Regulation, Accreditation, and Continuous Readiness.*

These modules feature critical components of healthcare quality, the science and art of quality and performance management, and environmental considerations such as healthcare reform. In addition, *Q Solutions* was developed using feedback from healthcare quality professionals and academic and policy experts in the field.

In our world of teeming technology, rapid innovation, and continuously expanding science, we also rely on hope day in and day out. We hope that political agendas will reflect the needs of patients, families, and other stakeholders; that resources will be available for the work to be done; and that fear will not result in barriers to uncovering mistakes, flaws, and failures. For healthcare quality to permeate the healthcare landscape, the cultures of silence that still exist in institutions must be eradicated.

In addition to emerging technologies and techniques, the foundation of our work involves the collaborative relationships we form and develop with various stakeholders. Our work, after all, is relationship based. Mutual respect and accord lead to mutual understanding and a sense of camaraderie as we face complex healthcare quality challenges. This is accomplished in many ways including affiliations with professional groups such as the National Association for Healthcare Quality (NAHQ).

Q Solutions is targeted to audiences across the care continuum and provides critical knowledge to develop and enhance essential leadership skills in healthcare quality. In effect, these tools and techniques are universal to any healthcare setting. The basic principles can be adapted to your organization. When we embarked on the third edition journey, there was no question about who the right people were to make these publications happen. We were humbled by the company we kept. Fortunately, these individuals made time for what proved to be a fruitful endeavor. The product you hold in your hands would not have been possible without the unceasing efforts of our esteemed authors—Cathy E. Duquette, PhD RN CPHQ NEA-BC; Robert Rosati, PhD; Susan V. White, PhD RN CPHQ NEA-BC FNAHQ; and Diane S. Brown, PhD RN CPHQ FNAHQ FAAN. Their vision for NAHQ is depicted on every page. We thank them all for their thoughts and ideas throughout the development process. In addition, we appreciate the thorough content examination by our external review panel members—James B. Conway, MS LFACHE; Gerald N. Glandon, PhD; John Hansen, MD MPH; Bernard J. Horak, PhD FACHE CPHQ; and Barbara G. Rebold, MS RN CPHQ. As always, we acknowledge the continuous support of the NAHQ Board of Directors, which has resulted in the successful launch of the third edition of *Q Solutions*.

The work of healthcare quality professionals is noble indeed. Armed with a set of advanced skills and practical tools, we are a force that can be boundless. Our nobility comes from the fact that we are truth seekers. We are constantly challenged to tell a quality story that is cogent, accurately depicts healthcare circumstances, and is understood by varying audiences. To be able to tell the truth, we must demand that healthcare organizations

- provide resources necessary to conduct investigations and to maintain reporting systems that use state-of-the-art information technologies;
- allow and support a solid infrastructure for continuous readiness, including health information technology that supports the continuous quality improvement paradigm and doesn't disappear after an accreditation survey or regulatory audit;
- ensure that all organizations are educated on the science of discovery (i.e., data, methods, analysis, and application); and
- contribute to the growing body of healthcare quality science by sharing evidence-based, outcomes-oriented quality techniques making a difference in the safety, care, and service embraced by forward-thinking, highly reliable organizations.

Our primary goal for this suite of *Q Solutions* modules is to provide NAHQ members and other quality and patient safety professionals with a product that is reliable, valid, innovative, and timely. These updated modules reflect recent changes in national healthcare safety as well as the transformation of healthcare as we know it. In the future, NAHQ plans to supplement these modules with other relevant topics and learning opportunities.

Luc R. Pelletier, MSN PMHCNS-BC CPHQ FNAHQ FAAN
San Diego, CA

Christy L. Beaudin, PhD LCSW CPHQ FNAHQ
Los Angeles, CA

About the Editors

Luc R. Pelletier, MSN PMHCNS-BC CPHQ FNAHQ FAAN, is an administrative liaison at Sharp Mesa Vista Hospital, a core adjunct faculty member at National University, and a healthcare consultant in San Diego, CA. He received a Master of Science degree in nursing from Yale University and a bachelor of science in nursing from Fairfield University. A healthcare quality professional for almost 25 years, Pelletier has participated in local and national initiatives that ensure safe and equitable care for behavioral health patients and has helped to shape systems of care and national standards of performance. He has published several books and written numerous chapters and peer-reviewed articles. He has delivered presentations on various nursing and healthcare quality topics and given writing seminars to aspiring authors. He was the editor in chief of the *Journal for Healthcare Quality* from 1998 to 2007. During his tenure, the journal grew in prominence as a leading healthcare quality publication and was the recipient of various publishing awards. He has served as a nurse expert with the U.S. Department of Justice and as a scientific consultant to the National Institutes of Health. His current research focus is on nurse residency programs in behavioral health and patient engagement. He is also a Fellow of the American Academy of Nursing and NAHQ.

Christy L. Beaudin, PhD LCSW CPHQ FNAHQ, is national director of quality for AIDS Healthcare Foundation in Los Angeles, CA. In her current role, Dr. Beaudin is responsible for healthcare safety, accreditation, infection prevention and control, public reporting, and education. At the executive level, she led healthcare safety efforts at Children's Hospital Los Angeles, PacifiCare Behavioral Health, and Value Behavioral Health, and served as vice president of research and development at Magellan Behavioral Health. Dr. Beaudin supported hospitals and managed care organizations in preparing for and maintaining state licensure and accreditation compliance including the National Committee for Quality Assurance (NCQA), URAC, Accreditation Association for Ambulatory Health Care (AAAHC), and The Joint Commission. Dr. Beaudin earned her doctorate in health services from the UCLA School of Public Health, master's degree in social work from San Diego State University, and bachelor's degree in criminal justice from California State University, San Bernardino. Dr. Beaudin is adjunct faculty at the University of Redlands and participates in state- and national-level quality initiatives for NAHQ, SNP Alliance, and the California HealthCare Foundation. She is widely published, serves on several editorial boards and review panels, and is a national subject matter expert on healthcare quality, behavioral health, and managed care.

About the Author

Susan V. White, PhD RN CPHQ NEA-BC FNAHQ, is the chief of quality management at the Orlando VA Medical Center in Orlando, FL. Her areas of responsibility include quality management, performance improvement, accreditation and continuous survey readiness, patient safety, risk management, peer review, infection control, and credentialing and privileging. Prior to this role, she was the associate chief nurse and quality improvement and magnet coordinator at the James A. Haley Veterans' Hospital in Tampa, FL, in addition to serving as the vice president of quality management of the Florida Hospital Association. She has an extensive career in healthcare in administrative and clinical roles. She was the associate executive director and director of nursing in a community hospital and developed the quality management program for a hospital within a large network. Dr. White received her master's degree in nursing as well as her doctorate in philosophy from the University of Florida. She is a member of multiple professional organizations including the Florida Association for Healthcare Quality (FAHQ), NAHQ, Florida Nurses Association (FNA), American Nurses Association (ANA), Florida Organization of Nurse Executives (FONE), American Organization of Nurse Executives (AONE), and Sigma Theta Tau. She is also the interviews editor for the *Journal for Healthcare Quality* (*JHQ*). She obtained status as a NAHQ Fellow in 2003 and received the NAHQ Claire Glover Quality Award in 2004, the state FAHQ Quality Award in 2004, and the FAHQ Author Award in 2007. Dr. White served as vice chair on the board of directors for the Florida Center for Nursing from its inception in 2001 until 2009, and was an initial member on the Florida Patient Safety Corporation, serving as vice chair. She has published widely and coedited *Patient Safety: Principles and Practices*, published by Springer Publishing in 2004.

External Review Board

This project could not have been completed without feedback from expert thought leaders in the healthcare quality industry. We thank Dr. Bernard J. Horak for providing feedback for this module.

Bernard J. Horak, PhD FACHE CPHQ
Professor and Program Director
Health Systems Administration
Georgetown University
Washington, DC

LEARNING OBJECTIVES

1. Establish priorities for quality and performance improvement (QPI) activities and develop action plans and projects.
2. Develop and provide survey preparation training (i.e., accreditation, licensure, or equivalent) and evaluate organizational readiness for external quality awards and recognition.
3. Develop evaluation planning, projects, activities, and selection of process and outcome measures.
4. Select and implement evidence-based practice guidelines (e.g., for standing orders or as guidelines for physician ordering practice) and critical pathways.
5. Design organizational QPI training (e.g., quality, patient safety) and provide training on QPI, program development, and evaluation.
6. Participate on QPI teams (i.e., as a team member, leader, or facilitator) and evaluate team performance.
7. Promote effective enterprise risk management strategies and leadership through organizational safety practices.
8. Communicate success (e.g., presentation, storyboards, and publications).

I. Establishing Priorities for Quality and Performance Improvement (QPI) Activities

The road to QPI begins with strategic planning. Through strategic planning, leaders identify priorities for the organization as well as potential areas for improvement, reflecting an integration of the strategies, resources, and performance goals. By narrowing the focus of the vision, leaders refine broad opportunities into specific priorities most amenable to action and change.

A. Definition and Importance

The environment surrounding healthcare organizations is *dynamic* (changes frequently) and *complex* (with many constituents). Since the mid-1990s, external forces in healthcare have become increasingly important with the focus on reform efforts and reduction in healthcare costs. The significant growth of managed care and its organizational entities (e.g., preferred provider organizations [PPOs], health maintenance organizations [HMOs], and preferred health organizations [PHOs]) and most recently accountable care organizations (ACOs), accompanied by a significant shift from the acute care hospital to subacute and ambulatory settings as a focus for delivery of care, has made strategic planning even more important. The most recent trend with "medical homes" has continued to shape healthcare, with more focus on health prevention, primary care, and care coordination.

Strategy is defined as "the plans and activities developed by an organization in pursuit of its goals and objectives, particularly in regard to positioning itself to meet external demands relative to its competition" (Shortell, Morrison, & Robbins, 1985, p. 220). Strategic planning is one way of coping with a dynamic and complex environment. The goals of strategic management (Ginter, Swayne, & Duncan, 2002) are to

- provide a framework for thinking about the business;
- create a fit between the organization and its external environment;
- provide a process for coping with change and organizational renewal;
- foster anticipation, innovation, and excellence;
- facilitate consistent decision making; and
- create organizational focus.

Quality has received a great deal of industry attention in recent years because organizations have come to realize that quality must be an integral part of the strategic plan.

B. Strategic Management Process

The strategic management process includes all the decisions and actions needed to meet the strategic goals. **Figure 1** shows the steps in the strategic management process. Before a strategy is formulated, leaders consider what they want to do, what they should do, and what they can do (Luthans, Hodgetts, & Thompson, 1990). Consideration of these three issues leads to the development of a strategic plan.

Figure 1. Strategic Management Process

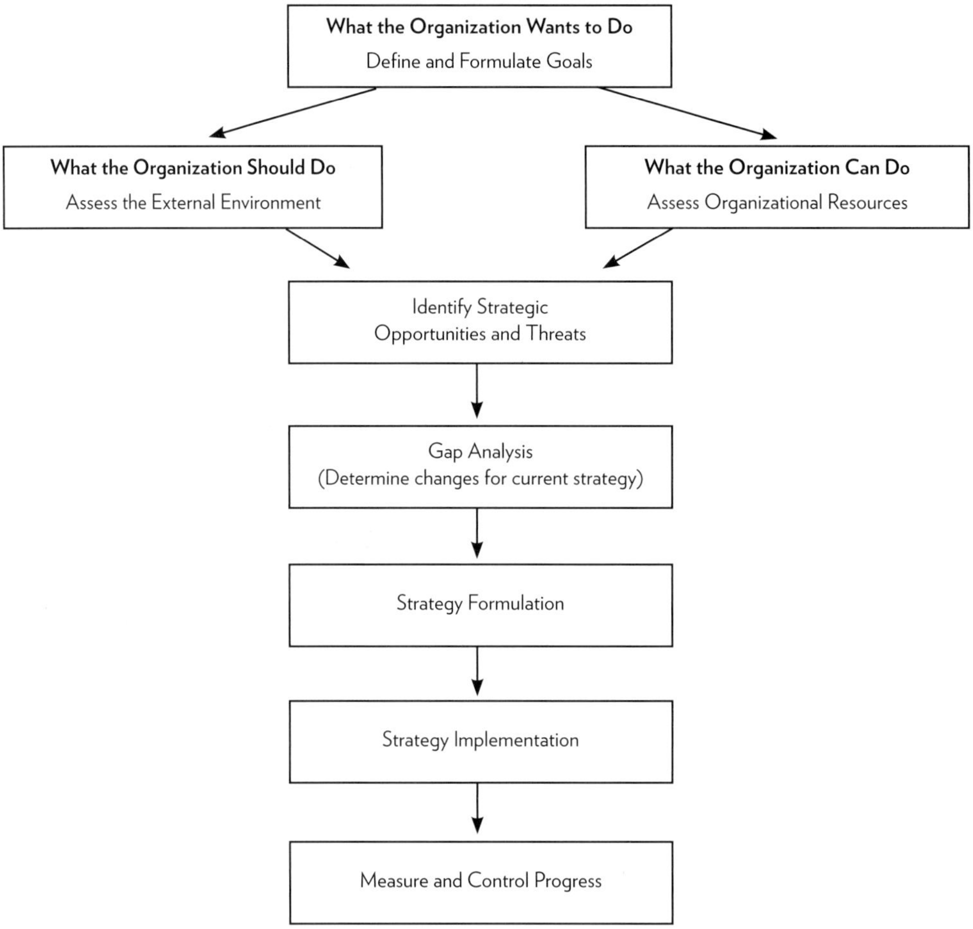

From Management, *by R. B. Dunham and J. L. Pierce, 1989, Glenview, IL: Scott Foresman and Company. Copyright 1989. Reprinted with permission.*

1. What the Organization Wants to Do

a. Mission and Vision

Organizations must define what they want to accomplish in the future. The *mission* is the organization's purpose or reason for existing. It answers questions such as, "Why are we here?" "Whom do we serve?" and "What do we do?" For example, the mission of SSM Health Care, a Malcolm Baldrige National Quality Award recipient, is "Through our exceptional healthcare services, we reveal the healing presence of God." Its core values are compassion, respect, excellence, stewardship, and community (SSM Health Care, 2005). This provides a long-term direction for the organization.

Vision is an organization's statement of its goals for the future, described in measurable terms that clarify the direction for everyone in the organization. An organization's direction is built on its mission and guided by its vision.

b. Guiding Principles and Core Values

Guiding principles define the organization's attitudes and policies for employees and thereby help to direct the vision. Customer focus is a core value central to any improvement initiative. The *customer* is the person or entity that receives the process, product, or service and therefore defines the quality of products or services received. The key to performance improvement is knowing and understanding the customer. The following list includes other core values contained in the Baldrige Health Care Criteria for Performance Excellence (Baldrige Performance Excellence Program, 2011–2012, p. 49):

- visionary leadership,
- patient-focused excellence,
- organizational and personal learning,
- valuing workforce members and partners,
- agility,
- focus on the future,
- managing for innovation,
- management by fact,
- societal responsibility and community health,
- focus on results and creating value, and
- system perspective.

c. Goals and Objectives

Goals and objectives are essential components of any planning process; they guide actions and serve as a yardstick for measuring the organization's progress and performance. Bill Hewlett, cofounder of Hewlett-Packard, once observed, "You cannot manage what you cannot measure . . . and what gets measured gets done" (House & Price, 1991, p. 93). There sometimes is confusion over the terms goal and objective; they differ with respect to scope and specificity. In general, goals are broad, general statements specifying a purpose or desired outcome and may be more abstract in nature than objectives (one goal can have several objectives).

Establishing goals is the initial step in the strategic planning process and sets the direction for the activities to follow. In general, goals need to be

- observable,
- measurable,
- challenging but attainable,
- controllable,
- visible, and
- time limited.

Objectives are specific statements that detail how the goals will be achieved; they therefore are more narrow and concrete. Objectives represent the organization's commitment to achieving specific outcomes. They should be written as action-oriented statements, outlining specific activities to be carried out and measurable and observable qualitative or quantitative performance outcomes. Examples of a mission statement, strategic goals, and strategic objectives can be found in **Table 1.**

Table 1. Example of Mission, Goals, and Objectives

Mission statement	We are a teaching hospital and critical member of the community, and our mission is to provide high-quality, innovative healthcare services to all members of our community regardless of race, religion, nationality, or ability to pay. We are dedicated to educating clients, with an emphasis on preventive healthcare.
Strategic goals	• Be recognized as one of the top healthcare providers in the community. • Establish an outreach program for management of chronic illness. • Develop a state-of-the-art program for breast cancer detection and treatment. • Reduce project costs by 15%.
Strategic objectives	• Hire highly skilled nursing staff and set minimum nurse-to-patient ratios to reduce staff turnover. • Obtain communication technology to allow distance education of clients and providers. • Provide education and time reimbursement for physicians to train in innovative breast cancer technology. • Control costs by using computerized planning tools (e.g., Program Evaluation Review Technique [PERT]).

The following are some general guidelines to use when writing objectives (Fisher & Samways, 1985):

- Keep the statements short and simple.
- State the end results or desired outcome and not just an activity.
- Specify the action to be taken, the condition under which the action is to be performed, and the criteria for successful completion.
- Write precisely to determine to what extent the objectives have been accomplished and what remains to be accomplished.
- Prioritize the objectives.

When goals are developed at the executive level, there must be corresponding goals and objectives for other levels in the organization, such as the business level and functional level (e.g., human resources, research and development) and the unit or departmental level (e.g., nursing, radiology, pharmacy). All levels should have both long-term and short-term goals and objectives. Another mnemonic for writing objectives is the SMART way (Specific, Measurable, Attainable, Relevant, and Time Bound; Centers for Disease Control and Prevention, 2011), which provides clear focus for developing a comprehensive way to ensure that objectives have all the necessary elements to be implemented and provide the guidance for the action plans needed for implementation.

2. What the Organization Should Do: Assessment of the External Environment

Once the objectives have been established (or revised), the organization must look at the external environment. On the roadmap, the environment is shown to influence what the organization wants to do. Because all organizations must adapt to the forces of the external environment to survive, stretch, and grow. In other words, the organization is one system among a variety of other systems in the external environment. Adaptation includes maintaining good relationships with key constituents who can influence its ability to meet the stated objectives. **Figure 2** depicts the various constituents whose needs must be met and balanced with the needs of other stakeholders. The outer ring represents the overall environment in which the organization exists. A variety of factors, including sociocultural, political and legal, economic, technological, global, and demographic forces, indirectly influence the organization. For example, economic forces can influence the amount of resources available to organizations (e.g., labor, capital). This is why organizations must scan the general

Figure 2. Potential Environmental Influences on QPI

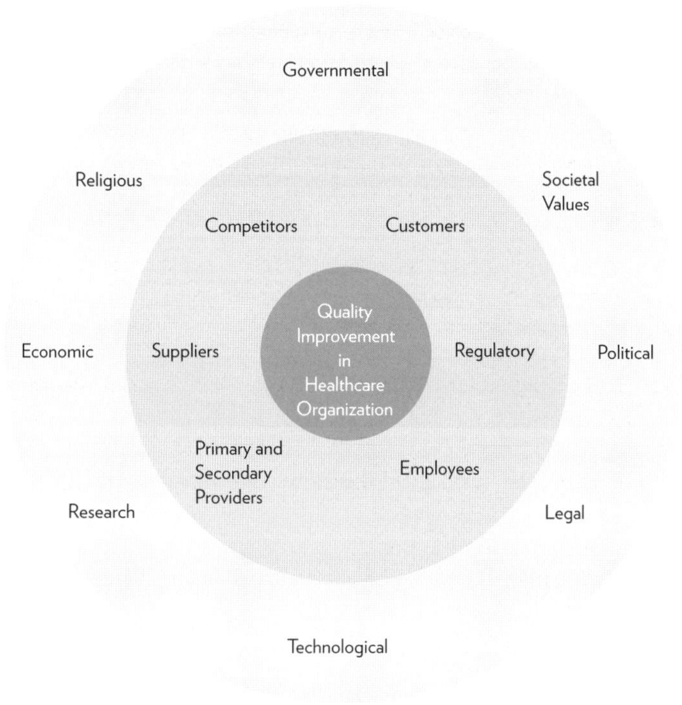

external environment looking for threats to, or opportunities for, meeting strategic goals and objectives. The second ring represents the immediate environment in which the organization operates. With respect to QPI, the key constituent is the customer. However, other constituents also are important. For example, the entity through which the patient acquires healthcare insurance (typically an employer), payers, and regulatory agencies also are key stakeholders.

3. What the Organization Can Do: Assessment of the Internal Environment

When the organization has established what it wants to do and what it should do based on assessment of the external environment, it needs to know what it can do. This requires an examination of the internal environment that looks at the resources, capabilities, and core competencies of the organization. Resources can be tangible (human, financial, physical) or intangible (reputation). For example, if an organization wants to be a leader in breast cancer detection and treatment, it must have qualified staff and equipment.

4. Strategy Formulation

Based on the strategic goals, objectives, and evaluation of external and internal environments, strategic opportunities and threats are identified. Generally, organizations perform a gap analysis to evaluate the extent to which the present strategy would have to be changed to meet the goals and objectives. Strategy formulation clearly stipulates actions to be taken to achieve goals. In the systems model (**Figure 3**), this is indicated by the arrows pointing to the lower half of the rectangle, describing the various subsystems in the organization that will undertake these actions to help the organization reach its goals.

Figure 3. Organizational Systems Model

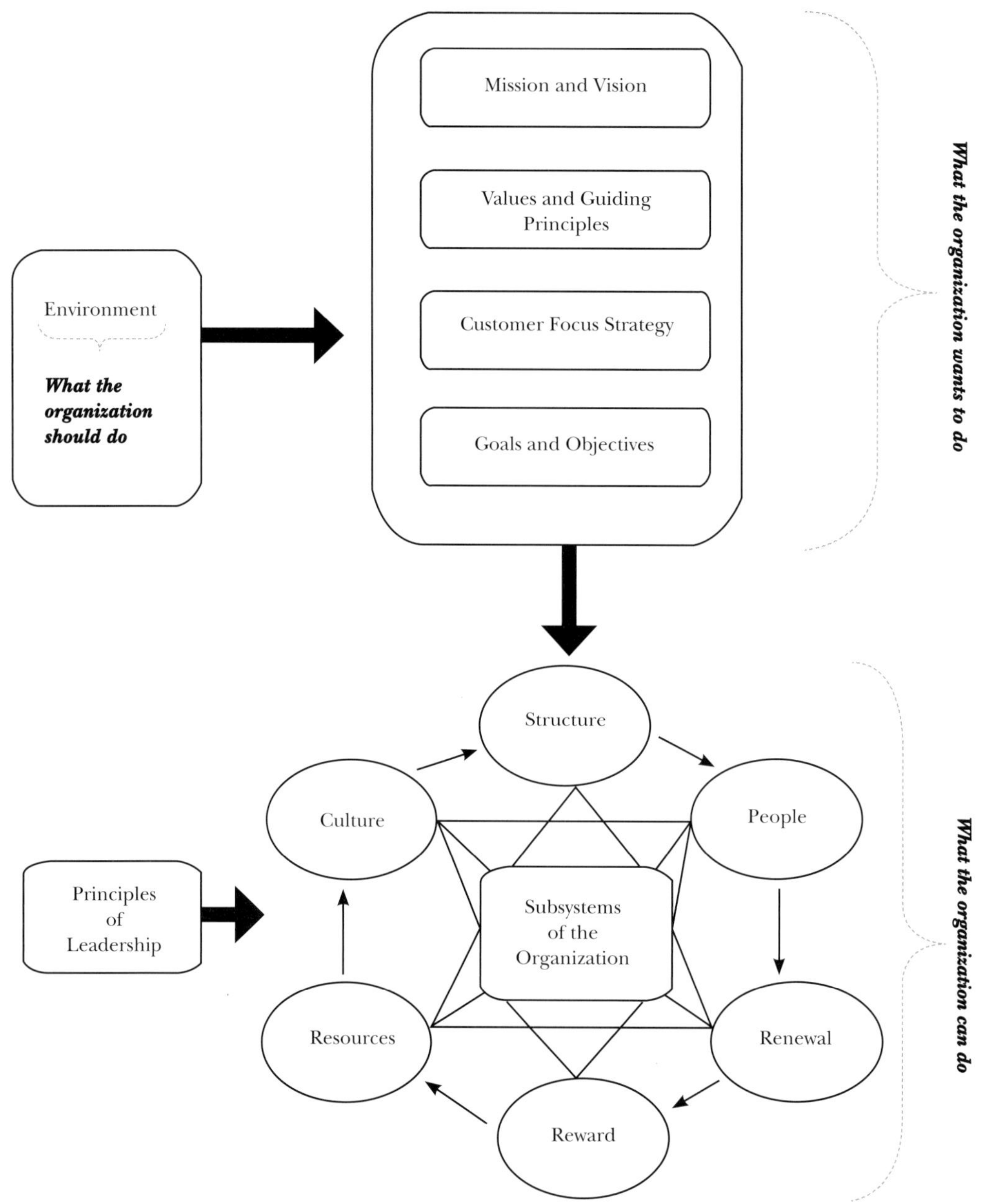

The organizational systems model depicted in Figure 3 builds on simpler models, further breaking down the elements and showing relationships between structure, process, and outcomes. The model begins at the top of the rectangle with formulation of mission, guiding principles, strategy, goals, and objectives; these give the organization direction and are the basis for strategy formulation. The "environment" box represents the multitude of stakeholders that must be satisfied, and the arrow demonstrates that the environment can influence the direction of the healthcare organization. Leadership is a critical process variable that influences the extent to which the structures (inputs) lead to desirable outcomes. The lower half of the diagram depicts subsystems of the organization or, in Donabedian's (1980) terms, *structural variables*. The lines connecting the various subsystems are meant to demonstrate that subsystems are interdependent. Changes in one subsystem typically mean that changes must also occur in other subsystems to keep them aligned. This conceptualization of subsystems was suggested by Peters and Waterman (1982) more than 30 years ago but remains just as applicable today.

5. Strategy Implementation

The various programs and departments develop their own strategies that will contribute to the overall goals and objectives of the organization. Top management can take a number of approaches to integrate QPI with strategic planning and to ensure that plans and strategies are being carried out. Hoshin planning (a Japanese term that means "policy deployment") is one approach for integration.

Hoshin planning is a component of the QPI system used to ensure that the vision set forth by top management is being translated into planning objectives and actions that both management and employees will take to accomplish long-term organizational strategic goals (**Figure 4**). "The primary reason to undertake Hoshin planning is to focus effort and resources on those few strategies and processes that will best achieve the organization's

Figure 4. Core Hoshin Planning Process

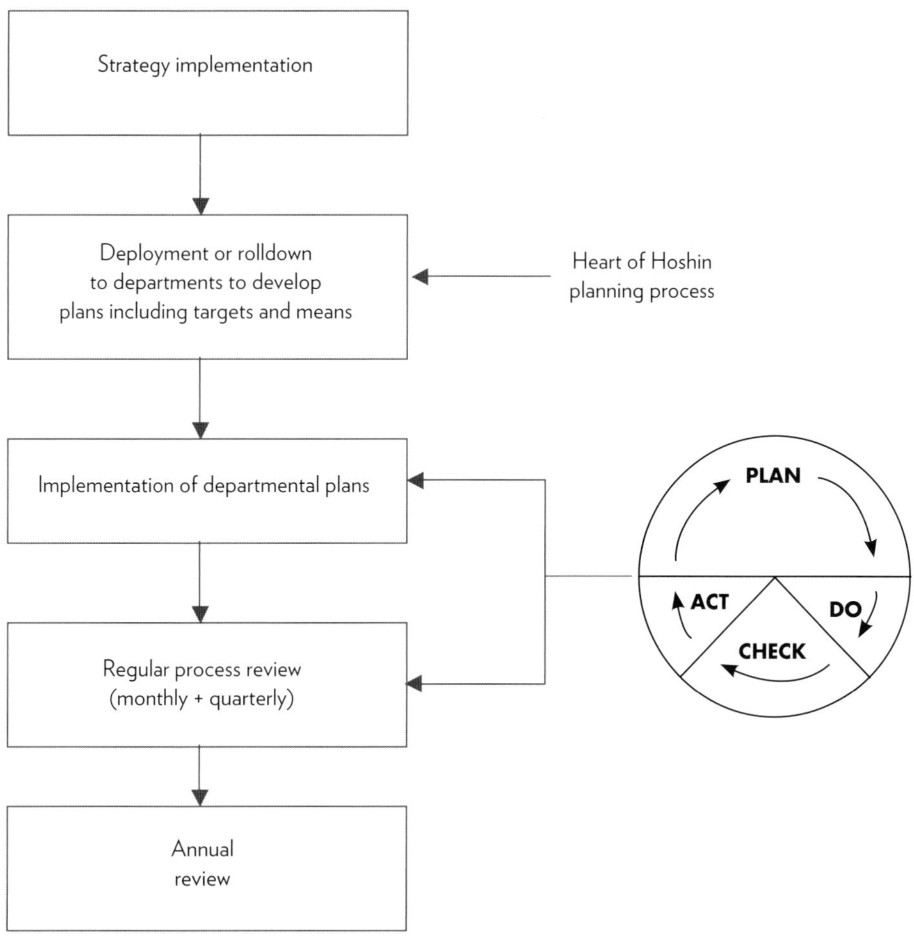

survival and vision, and to develop an effective process to align the goals and efforts of the organization" (Gaucher & Coffey, 1993, p. 492). The planning typically is performed at three levels: general (senior management), intermediate (middle management), and detailed (implementation teams). Furthermore, the Hoshin concept is based on the principle that high-performance organizations are those that harness the creative-thinking power of all of its employees. In this model, each employee is regarded as the expert at their own job and their contributions are consistently acknowledged (Hutchins, 2008).

II. Translating Strategic Goals into Quality Outcomes

A. The Governing Body's Role in QPI

The organization's governing body bears ultimate responsibility for setting policy, financial and strategic direction, and the quality of care and service provided by all of its practitioners. Together with the organization's management and medical staff leaders, the governing body sets priorities for QPI activities.

The development of meaningful governing body involvement in QPI requires assessment of the governing body's knowledge of QPI. This is a key role of healthcare quality professionals, who are responsible for organizing and coordinating quality management and performance improvement activities for the organization and its medical staff. Healthcare quality professionals can promote the governing body's commitment to quality by providing useful information in a format easily understood by members who may lack familiarity with healthcare terminology and procedures.

The American Hospital Association (AHA, 1999) has outlined Principles of Accountability for Hospitals and Healthcare Organizations, with specific directives for governing board and leadership. These government and leadership directives are described in **Table 2**.

For practical purposes, day-to-day leadership is delegated to the CEO and senior management, elected or appointed members of the medical staff (e.g., chairs), and administrative and clinical staff (e.g., healthcare quality professionals).

B. Fundamental Principles of Leadership

Leadership is the ability to influence an individual or group toward achievement of goals (Robbins, 2001). Leadership and management are not identical. *Leadership* is determining the correct direction or path, whereas *management* is doing the correct things to stay on that path. Kotter (1990) notes that management is about coping with complexity through planning and budgeting; setting goals; organizing, staffing, and creating a structure to foster goal attainment; setting up mechanisms for monitoring; and controlling results. In contrast, leaders are responsible for coping with change by developing a vision for change and aligning the subsystems of the organization. Both strong leadership and management are necessary for high performance. Some people are great leaders but poor managers and vice versa; in some cases, a person may be successful in both roles.

C. Leadership Framework

There are many frameworks for leadership. As is true with the system framework, often it is less important to choose a particular framework than simply to have one to guide behavior. Deming (2000) believed that managers were responsible for optimizing the system. According to the model in Figure 3, "optimizing" would involve aligning the subsystems of the organization. What types of leadership practices are essential to this process?

Table 2. AHA's Principles of Accountability for Hospitals and Healthcare Organizations: Governance/Leadership

Mission and Vision. The organization's governing body and leadership should articulate clearly defined mission and vision statements. With these statements as a foundation, the organization's leadership should develop an action plan with specific goals, time frames for accomplishment, and linked measures of performance for a regular assessment of achievement, with oversight by the governing body. As part of this development process, the organization's governing body and leadership should seek input from relevant stakeholders concerning their needs and interests relative to the organization. The plan and the results should be widely communicated to all individuals who are employed by or affiliated with the organization.

Executive Management Oversight. The organization's governing body is responsible for the oversight of the organization's leadership performance and should periodically evaluate that performance relative to the organization's achievement of its stated strategic goals. As part of the process of evaluating the organization's leadership, the governing body should periodically and systematically assess its own performance relative to defined goals and measures of performance.

Quality Oversight. The organization's governing body and leadership, in conjunction with the clinical staff, are responsible for developing and implementing, in a comprehensive manner, systems and procedures for safeguarding and enhancing the quality of patient care and services. The governing body and leadership, in conjunction with the clinical staff, are also responsible for actively monitoring and immediately acting upon, where appropriate, the results derived from those systems and procedures such that patient and staff safety is ensured or improvements in patient care occur.

Financial Stability. The organization's governing body is responsible for ensuring the financial well-being of the organization and, in conjunction with the organization's leadership, for overseeing the appropriate and most optimal allocation of financial and physical resources for the improvement of patient care. The organization's mission and duty to improve patient care and community health must not be obstructed by (and must take precedence over) the financial interests of individuals or groups employed by or affiliated with the organization.

From Accountability—The Pathway to Restoring Public Trust and Confidence for Hospitals and Other Health Care Organizations, *p. 8, November 11-12, 1999, by the American Hospital Association, Chicago, IL: AHA. Copyright 1999. Reprinted with permission.*

Practices of exemplary leaders were explored by Kouzes and Posner (2002), who identified five important general practices: inspire a shared vision, challenge the system, enable others to act, model the way, and encourage the heart. These principles are generic and therefore applicable to any type of organization.

Inspire a Shared Vision. For any change to be successful, leaders must provide a vision for QPI and influence people to share that vision. This means getting people to accept the core values underlying QPI by developing a strong culture.

Challenge the System. Challenging the system means acting as a change agent for that vision. It also means recognizing good ideas and demonstrating a willingness to stretch and grow to improve the quality of care. This, too, involves adoption of core values as a learning organization.

Enable Others to Act. The third leadership practice is enabling others to act by sharing decision making and power. Along with sharing power, enabling involves having an appropriate structural design and resources to support QPI initiatives.

Model the Way. Much behavior is learned through role modeling. Leaders who expect employees to make changes to support QPI must model those desired behaviors; actions speak louder than words.

Encourage the Heart. The last practice is critical. Change is difficult, even if it is done for the right reasons. Encouraging the heart means recognizing contributions employees make and celebrating the core values and victories. The most important point of any reward system is to reward the desired behaviors.

Leaders use these five practices to keep subsystems aligned. However, leaders must first get people to support a vision of quality. One way this occurs is through a strong culture of QPI.

III. Aligning Culture to Support Quality

A. Definition and Importance of Culture

Culture has been defined as the social glue that holds people together (Siehl & Martin, 1981). At the heart of culture is the notion of shared values (what is important) and behavioral norms (the way things are done; Rokeach, 1973). Cultures are described as strong when the core values are intensely held and widely shared. Strong culture

- provides a sense of identity for employees and commitment to something larger than themselves;
- enhances cooperation;
- creates a system of informal rules spelling out how people are expected to behave; and
- creates distinctions between organizations, allowing a definite competitive advantage to develop.

B. Elements of Culture

Culture has both hidden and visible elements. Hidden elements are values and norms, whereas visible elements include symbols; language, slogans, and brands; ritual and ceremonies; stories, legends, and myths; and heroes.

Values and Norms. The core values reflected in the Baldrige Performance Excellence Program are one example. The role of leaders is to inspire commitment to these underlying quality values.

Symbols. Symbols are things that represent an idea. The purpose of symbols is to reflect the culture, trigger values and norms, and help people make sense of their organization. For example, one hospital wanted to strengthen the value for reporting adverse events. To do this, staff wore buttons that said, "We care, We report, We learn."

Language, Slogans, and Brands. Language and slogans are intended to convey cultural meaning to employees and stakeholders. They should be easy to learn, remember, and repeat (e.g., "Quality is Job 1," "Thrive"). Brands help build loyalty to a product or service.

Rituals and Ceremonies. Rituals and ceremonies reinforce an organization's core values and goals, thereby strengthening culture.

Stories, Legends, and Myths. Stories, legends, and myths are narrative examples repeated by employees to inform (often new) employees about culture. Stories are based on fact; legends are based on facts but embellished; myths are consistent with the culture but are not based on fact.

Heroes. Heroes are company role models whose ideals, character, and support of the organizational culture highlight the values and norms a company wants to reinforce. Heroes provide a role model for success. By design or default, an organization develops a culture. It is better to actively direct the evolution of that culture than to try to change a strong culture that is not aligned with the goals of QPI.

C. Assessing Culture

How can it be determined whether performance improvement (PI) is a core value in an organization? In a model proposed by Schein (1992) and Schneider (1990), the following questions can assess the culture of PI:

- Does the leader pay attention to, measure, and control quality on a regular basis?
- Are scarce resources allocated to PI?
- Are behaviors supporting PI rewarded?
- Do staff knowledge, skills, and behaviors important for PI figure into decisions about recruitment, selection, and promotion?

- Is active involvement in PI activities one measure of status in the organization?
- Are people spending time on PI?
- Does staff frequently discuss PI?
- Is the prevailing attitude toward PI positive or negative?

D. Strengthening Culture for QPI

Many actions for strengthening a quality culture flow from the aforementioned questions. First, leaders must show visible support through such actions as

- making QPI everyone's responsibility,
- having an annual budget for QPI,
- making QPI part of the strategic planning process, and
- rewarding behaviors that support QPI.

Second, the visible elements of culture must receive attention. For example, the following must be accomplished.

- Old, negative stories about QPI that are acting as barriers to cultural change must be replaced with new, positive ones.
- Symbols to reinforce values critical to quality must be created. Rituals that reinforce values critical to quality must be established.
- Leaders must celebrate successes relating to QPI.

Finally, leaders must be persistent. Culture takes a long time to change (see *Q Solutions: Healthcare Safety*).

Although inspiring people to a vision is critical, leaders must also enable others to achieve goals and objectives. One way to enable others is to structure or design the organization in a way that supports QPI.

IV. Aligning Structure to Support Quality

A. Definition and Importance

Designing an organization is similar to designing a house.

> *Like the physical structure of a house, organizational structure identifies and distinguishes the individual parts of an organization and ties these pieces together to define an integrated whole. Organizational structure differs from the physical structure of a house, however, in that it encompasses more than inanimate characteristics of walls, doors, and windows. Organizational structure includes the interaction patterns that link people to people and people to work, and unlike a house, structural dimensions of organizations frequently change and evolve. (Dunham & Pierce, 1989, p. 399)*

Choices for applying resources for performance improvement and quality measurement are based on organizational priorities, available resources, and other drivers such as social, political, and regulatory requirements. As a matter of policy and practical considerations, accreditation standards alone do not address outcomes directly. First, there were problems with the way quality was measured. Second, no professional consensus existed on systematic measures of patient outcomes. Finally, uniform and comparable clinical databases were nonexistent.

The problem of measuring and interpreting patient outcomes precluded practical use in accreditation. As a consequence, the accreditation process was necessarily built on an implicit assumption that if proper structures and processes were in place, good outcomes were likely to follow. The Joint Commission and other accreditation organizations have since moved into using other mechanisms for assessing processes and outcomes, such as individual patient tracers and second-generation tracers, which focus on specific areas such as disinfection and sterilization, credentialing and privileging, information systems, and radiation dosing. Although the Joint Commission is the largest healthcare accreditation organization, it is not alone; other organizations provide accreditation to healthcare organizations for general care and specialty care (**Table 3**).

Table 3. Healthcare Accreditation Organizations

Accreditation Body	Primary Focus of Accreditation
Accreditation Association for Ambulatory Health Care (AAAHC)	Ambulatory healthcare organizations, including ambulatory surgery centers, office-based surgery centers, endoscopy centers, and college student health centers, as well as managed care organizations, such as health maintenance organizations and preferred provider organizations
Accreditation Commission for Health Care (ACHC)	Home care, hospice and durable medical equipment, prosthetics, orthotics, and supplies (DMEPOS)
American Board for Certification in Orthotics, Prosthetics & Pedorthics (ABC)	Comprehensive orthotics and prosthetics, pedorthics, ocular prosthetics, mastectomy, noncustom therapeutic footwear, DMEPOS
American College of Radiology (ACR) Accreditation	Breast magnetic resonance imaging, breast ultrasound, computed tomography, mammography, magnetic resonance imaging, nuclear medicine and positron emission tomography, radiation oncology, stereotactic breast biopsy, ultrasound
American Osteopathic Association (AOA) Healthcare Facilities Accreditation Program	Healthcare facilities, predoctoral and postdoctoral training programs, hospitals and clinical laboratories
CARF International	Aging services; behavioral health; business and service management networks; CARF/Continuing Care Accreditation Commission (CCAC); child and youth services; DMEPOS; employment and community services; medical rehabilitation; opioid treatment programs; vision rehabilitation services
College of American Pathologists Accreditation and Laboratory Improvement	Laboratory services, biorepository program, reproductive program, forensic drug testing
Community Health Accreditation Program (CHAP)	Community-based healthcare organizations
Det Norske Veritas (DNV International Accreditation) National Integrated Accreditation for Healthcare Organizations (NIAHO)	Healthcare organizations (clinical, management, and environmental safety); leading accreditor of U.S. hospitals integrating ISO 9001 quality compliance with the Medicare Conditions of Participation.
Healthcare Quality Association on Accreditation (HQAA)	Home and durable medical equipment
National Committee for Quality Assurance (NCQA)	Individual physicians, health plans, medical groups, disease management (uses Healthcare Effectiveness Data and Information Set [HEDIS] and Consumer Assessment of Healthcare Providers and Systems [CAHPS] data)
American Society of Health-System Pharmacists (ASHP) Accreditation	Residency accreditation, pharmacy technician accreditation
The Joint Commission	Healthcare organizations: hospitals, critical access hospitals, ambulatory care, long-term care, behavioral health, home care, laboratory services, special diseases and conditions
URAC	Health plan, health network, and utilization management

1. Survey Preparation

Continuous survey readiness (CSR) is the goal rather than ramp-up process, although there is often final preparation for any survey. However, because most surveys are unannounced, the CSR model is ideal. First, one must clearly understand the applicable standards, criteria, or survey requirements. Then training preparation begins, with a focus on the audience. Content experts need ongoing training and education to lead the survey readiness process and train others. Management staff need education and training to ensure that their department or service is ready by developing policies, processes, and other organizational guidance. Staff members need very specific training to ensure that they implement the standards, policies, and processes into daily work.

Because CSR must be an ongoing process, a variety of approaches and learning methods should be used, including the following:

- face-to-face education,
- rounds of work areas with environment assessment and staff knowledge assessment,
- questions and answer tools (daily, weekly, and monthly),
- resource books of common standards updated at least annually,
- self-assessment tools to identify gaps in comparison to standards and education and other action plans to address the gaps,
- visual tools or cognitive aids such as posters on safety goals or performance improvement model,
- content experts to respond one-on-one to questions or interpretation of standards,
- tools for tracer activities, and
- mock surveys to assess compliance with standards in an ongoing manner.

An extensive discussion on regulation, accreditation and continuous readiness can be found in *Q Solutions: Regulation, Accreditation, and Continuous Readiness.*

2. Facilitating the Credentialing and Privileging Process

Medical staff members of an organization provide patient care and fulfill other professional responsibilities through rules and defined policies. The bylaws and rules of the medical staff are documents that delineate how the medical staff will organize and govern its affairs. The essential components include the following:

- structure and membership of the medical staff;
- credentialing function;
- processes for appointment and for granting clinical privileges;
- provisional period for initial appointment;
- reappraisal or reappointment process;
- responsibilities of department chairpersons, department, and chief of staff;
- fair hearings and due process; and
- mechanisms for corrective action.

The two components of allowing members of the medical staff to practice and provide patient care within an organization are credentialing and privileging. These two components will be described separately.

Credentialing Process. The term *credentialing* refers to the systematic process of screening and evaluating qualifications and other credentials, including licensure, required education, relevant training and experience, and current competence and health status of a member of the medical staff. This applies to licensed independent practitioners (LIPs) as well as certain other professionals who may or may not be LIPs but are members of the medical staff with either privileges or a scope of practice. The credentials of the licensed professional must be verified through primary source verification. Primary source verification is documentation from the original source of a specific credential that verifies the accuracy of a qualification reported by an individual healthcare practitioner. This can be documented in the form of a letter, documented telephone contact, or secure electronic communication with the original source. The organization is responsible for this process to ensure that anyone providing patient care truly has the credentials presented and that there are no adverse actions against the provider.

The following items are minimally verified for each LIP:

- current licensure, which is the official or legal permission to practice in an occupation, as evidenced by documentation issued by a state, territory, commonwealth, or the District of Columbia in the form of a license, registration, or certification;
- education from an accredited program with evidence of successful graduation;
- board certification (if required);
- training (any specialized training such as fellowships);
- references from peers;
- medical malpractice claims;
- reports to the National Practitioner Data Bank (NPDB) and Healthcare Integrity and Protection Data Bank (HIPDB); and
- current competence.

The credentialing (and privileging) process is repeated every 2 years with updated information to ensure that the practitioner maintains current credentials and competence to provide safe, high-quality care.

Privileging Process. The privileging process is based on the services provided at the organization and approved by the medical staff. The practitioner's qualifications and request for privileges are considered based on the procedures and types of services and care that can be provided by the organization. The practitioner requests privileges based on his or her education, training, and experience, and then the clinical department makes recommendations to the medical staff through the medical executive committee. Privileges are granted by the organization through the committee's recommendations to the governing body. The term *clinical privileging* is defined as the process by which a practitioner, licensed for independent practice (e.g., without supervision, direction, required sponsor, preceptor, mandatory collaboration), is permitted by law and the facility to practice independently to provide specified medical or other patient care services within the scope of the practitioner's license, based on his or her clinical competence as determined by peer references, professional experience, health status, education, training, and licensure. Clinical privileges must be facility- and provider-specific. Credentialing and privileging of dependent and independent practitioners are outlined in **Table 4**. Clinical privileges may be defined several ways and categorized by

- practitioner specialty,
- level of training and experience,
- patient risk categories,
- lists of procedures or treatments, and
- any combination of the above.

At the time of the initial appointment to the medical staff, the practitioner must complete a Focused Professional Practice Evaluation (FPPE). The FPPE is a time-limited process whereby the organization evaluates and confirms the current competence of the

Table 4. Comparison of Dependent and Independent Practitioners for Credentialing and Privileging

Aspect	Dependent Practitioner	Independent Practitioner
Credentials	Required licensure, education, and certification if applicable	Required licensure, any action against licensure, education from accredited program, special training (such as fellowship), board eligibility or certification if required, peer references, malpractice history
Description of function	Job description	Privileges (or scope of practice)
Brought on to the organization	Hired	Appointed
Probationary period	Initial competence assessment (often a skills checklist)	Initial competence is assessed by Focused Professional Practice Evaluation (FPPE).
Ongoing development	Education and training within profession	Education and training within profession
Reassessment of competence	Regular ongoing competence assessment (period defined by the organization and accreditation standards)	Competence is reassessed by Ongoing Professional Practice Evaluation (OPPE).
Evaluation	Annual performance evaluation	OPPE is used for consideration of reappointment (time frame is every 2 years).
Performance issues (clinical)	A personal improvement plan to correct deficiencies	An OPPE or other triggers may require an FPPE for cause.
Ongoing review	Continued employment with the organization	Reappointment to the medical staff

practitioner's performance for all initially requested privileges or when issues affecting the provision of safe, effective patient care are identified. This process usually includes an assessment for proficiency in the following six areas of general competencies developed by the Accreditation Council for Graduate Medical Education (ACGME) and the American Board of Medical Specialties (ABMS) joint initiative:

- patient care,
- medical or clinical knowledge,
- practice-based learning and improvement,
- interpersonal and communication skills,
- professionalism, and
- systems-based practice.

After the initial FPPE is completed, the practitioner's performance is monitored in an ongoing manner through the Ongoing Professional Practice Evaluation (OPPE). The OPPE is a process that continuously evaluates a practitioner's professional performance to identify problems that may affect quality of care and patient safety. Ongoing provider evaluation is an evidence-based privilege renewal process and is part of a decision-making process that is used on a biennial basis to continue a provider's existing privileges or scope of practice or to limit or revoke existing privileges or scope of practice before or at the time of renewal. This process includes an assessment of proficiency in the six ACGME areas of general competency. Other criteria that may be used by an organization depending on services provided include the following:

- patterns of blood and pharmaceutical usage,
- use of tests and procedures,
- length-of-stay patterns,
- morbidity and mortality data,
- use of consultants,
- performance measures,
- medical record management,
- periodic and retrospective chart reviews,
- direct observation,
- monitoring of diagnostic and treatment techniques,
- compliance with policies,
- review of operative and other clinical procedures performed and their outcomes, and
- other service-specific items.

The reprivileging process occurs simultaneously with recredentialing every 2 years during a reappraisal. This is conducted at the time of reappointment to medical staff or renewal or revision of clinical privileges. Renewal is based on ongoing monitoring of information—OPPE—and includes confirmation of adherence to medical staff membership requirements, rules and regulations, and policies. Through the OPPE, medical staff leaders consider relevant practitioner-specific information, results of peer review, and other performance evaluations. The governing body is ultimately responsible for the credentialing and privileging process and the quality of care provided by members of the medical staff. The processes are usually managed by staff in the medical staff office or QPI department. Regardless of where the function is housed, it must include the following processes:

- initial appointments;
- reappointments;
- granting, renewing, and expanding clinical privileges; and
- fair hearing and appeal in the event of an adverse decision on granting, revoking, revising, or renewing clinical privileges for medical staff members or others holding clinical privileges in accordance with applicable statutes, rights of the individuals, and bylaws.

The organization maintains a credential file for each person requesting clinical privileges. A separate OPPE file includes performance data reviewed by the department medical staff chair. Credential files contain clear evidence that the full range of privileges has been included in the initial and subsequent reappraisals, particularly privileges for performing high-risk procedures and treating high-risk conditions. Information is substantive and practitioner-specific. The effectiveness of the reappraisal process may be measured by objective documentation that the individual's privileges were increased, reduced, or terminated because of

- assessments of documented performance,
- nonuse of privileges for high-risk procedures or treatments, and
- emergence of new technologies.

Under specific situations, temporary privileges for a defined period of time may be granted after minimal criteria are verified. Also, disaster privileges may be granted if the organization determines it will allow them and specific criteria are met.

The healthcare quality professional must abide by the standards set by accrediting agencies and state professional boards regarding credentialing and privileging processes.

3. Overview of QPI

Definitions and requirements for quality in healthcare have evolved over the past decades. In the early 1950s, quality care review was conducted exclusively by individual physicians using an unstructured and subjective process that relied on the practitioner's knowledge and experiences. Between 1950 and 1960, the responsibility for quality of care expanded beyond the physician to include both the hospital and the board of directors. Two significant legal decisions marked this transition period:

- *Bing v. Thunig* (1957). In this case, the New York Court of Appeals ruled that the doctrine of charitable immunity no longer applied to hospitals; hospitals are liable for patient injuries sustained through negligence of employees.
- *Darling v. Charleston Community Memorial Hospital* (1965). In this important corporate negligence case, the court ruled that the hospital had a legal responsibility to protect a patient from harm by others by overseeing the quality of patient care.

B. Retrospective Audits

A shift from physician review to medical audits occurred in 1955. Medical audits included a systematic procedure using objective, valid criteria with an orientation on outcomes. In 1966 there was a major change whereby the Joint Commission on Accreditation of Hospitals (as it was called then; now the Joint Commission) focused on optimal, not minimal, standards of care. In 1975, the Joint Commission on Accreditation of Hospitals published the quality of professional services standards, requiring hospitals to demonstrate optimal care using valid and reliable measures. Although *optimal* was never defined, this new focus led to one-time audits of care, known as performance evaluation programs audits.

C. Quality Assurance

Audits soon led to a preoccupation with meeting audit number requirements. As a result, in 1980 the Joint Commission on Accreditation of Hospitals developed the first quality assurance standards requiring a problem-focused approach to measuring quality. This approach required organizations to identify and monitor problem areas.

The combined strengths of criteria-based audits and the epidemiological approach used in infection control in the 1980s resulted in a new focus on systematic monitoring and evaluation in 1985. From this, a 10-step process for QPI evolved in 1986 requiring organizations to evaluate important aspects of care and then use the results to identify opportunities for improvement.

D. QPI Method

By the early 1990s QPI methods were becoming common in healthcare facilities. In 1994, the Joint Commission on Accreditation of Healthcare Organizations (JCAHO) introduced the new standards for improving organizational performance, requiring a collaborative culture that focuses on processes by elucidating how customers define quality, how processes work, and the importance of reducing variation in those processes (JCAHO, 1994). This represents a shift in focus from the performance of individuals to the performance of the organization's systems and processes. There is no longer any department-specific review (e.g., no ancillary services review for QPI); QPI is reviewed for the entire organization (JCAHO, 1994). The standards also required a shift from improving only clinical quality to improving nonclinical care, value, and patient satisfaction.

The following discussion on performance management centers on the organizational level in the context of meeting the organization's strategic goals and objectives.

E. Performance Management

Performance management has been defined as "the use of performance management information to effect positive change in organizational culture, systems, and processes by helping to set agreed-upon performance goals, allocating and prioritizing resources, informing managers to either confirm or change current policy or program direction to meet those goals, and sharing results of performance in pursuing those goals" (U.S. Department of Energy, Office of Management, n.d.). The goal of a performance management system is to make certain that the vision of the organization is being met by defining and measuring outcomes reflected in that vision.

Although there are a variety of quality performance programs, including the Baldrige Performance Excellence Program and the European Foundation for Quality Management, a significant percentage of government agencies and Fortune 1000 companies use the balanced scorecard (BSC) as an approach to performance management. BSCs are completely compatible with other quality performance programs but go beyond such programs by embedding QPI in the strategic framework of the organization (Kaplan & Bower, 2001).

The BSC was developed by Drs. David Norton and Robert Kaplan in the early 1990s. The basic idea is that performance measures should provide a comprehensive view of organizational performance and not be overly dependent on a few choice indicators. Unlike other performance models, the BSC helps organizations better link long-term strategy with short-term activities (Kaplan & Norton, 1996).

The BSC approach views the organization from four different perspectives or categories: financial ("How do we look to providers of financial resources?"), customer ("How do our customers see us?"), internal business processes ("At what must we excel?"), and learning and growth ("Can we continue to improve and create value for customers?"). Answers to these questions influence the nature of the strategic goals and objectives that are set and, ultimately, what performance measures are used. The critical aspect of performance indicators is that they must reflect the organization's strategic goals and objectives.

There are likely to be several strategic objectives corresponding to each of the four perspectives. Each of these objectives should have at least one measure, and the principles described in *Q Solutions: Leadership and Management* regarding measure precision, reliability, validity, and mixture of qualitative and quantitative all hold true here. In addition, data can be collected through a variety of means (e.g., surveys, focus groups, patient chart reviews).

Kelly (2003) suggests that development and use of different types of measures (i.e., structure, process, outcomes) in each of the categories is an important approach. Examples of the four categories and measures in the context of the strategic goals and objectives discussed earlier (Table 1) are presented next.

The foundation for an organization's strategic success begins with its people, who must be willing to learn and grow. To meet the changing needs of customers, they must, for example, be able to learn new technology and acquire new skills in order to take on new responsibilities. For the strategic goal "Develop a state-of-the-art program for breast cancer detection and treatment" (see Table 1), measures could include

- structure: quantity of imaging equipment;
- process: number of patients diagnosed with imaging technology; and
- outcome: higher percentage of early diagnoses, due to use of imaging technology.

It is necessary to monitor and improve key processes so that employees are able to convert learning and growth into products and services or quality outcomes. "Be recognized as one of the top healthcare providers in the community" was another strategic goal (see Table 3). Measures could include

- structure: resources available for care delivery (e.g., nurse–patient ratio);
- process: care (how patients are diagnosed and treated); and
- outcomes: results of care (e.g., satisfaction, length and quality of life, turnover rates).

Just as different organizational levels and units develop goals and objectives based on corporate strategy, different levels and units also can use BSC. Also, note that for the same strategic goal (e.g., be recognized as one of the top healthcare providers in the community) there are several measures of performance across different perspectives.

F. Setting Priorities for QPI

The road to QPI begins with strategic planning to guide the organization in focusing on the most important aspects or priorities. Priorities for performance or QPI activities are based on several standard approaches. The first approach is that the priorities should be aligned with the organization's strategic priorities in order to maximize resources for improvement, and the second is a criteria-based approach considering risk, volume, problem proneness, patient safety, cost, customer satisfaction, and other criteria established specifically by the organization. The pillars identified by Quint Studer are also often used as the categories of improvement priorities: Service, Quality, Financial, People, and Growth (Studer Group, 2012).

A framework for leadership of improvement is the first step in turning the strategic plan into an operational plan for improvement. In this framework leaders apply the mission, vision, values, and strategic plan to set direction. This framework is built on a foundational leadership team to support improvement capability. The three components of *will to prepare for change, ideas to generate new ways of performing,* and *execution of change* contribute to a leadership system for improvement. This model is depicted in **Figure 5**. A detailed view of this framework is presented in **Figure 6**. Finally, this framework is presented as an integrated system in **Figure 7**.

G. Priorities for QPI

Prioritizing evaluates key processes against key business drivers to identify the most important processes to improve and measure in evaluating performance. Applying priorities determines the initiation of an improvement action, based on the analysis of data collection. The goals and drivers of the system are depicted in **Figure 8**. Leaders identify a priority list of processes or services for improvement (Provost, Miller, & Reinertsen, 2006). Healthcare quality professionals facilitate development of priorities by

- establishing criteria for priority assessment (e.g., volume, risk, problem proneness),
- using data on past performance to assess gaps (internal performance),
- using external drivers for consideration (new regulations, standards),
- providing information to leaders with a basis for recommendations,
- using tools to create a matrix for priorities for decision making,
- involving key stakeholders for input, and
- identifying internal and external requirements that influence priorities.

In addition, healthcare quality professionals and their QPI teams use the described criteria to prioritize QPI activities based on the quantitative and qualitative data available to them. By using past performance, aligned with the criteria and strategic initiatives, the team is able to determine the priorities for action. A plan should be established that is approved by the clinical leaders to ensure success of the activities, especially in applying resources for the effort required for the team. The initiatives that have the most opportunity for improvement are often tackled first. Usually, the initiatives selected will focus on core clinical processes,

Figure 5. Framework for Leadership of Improvement

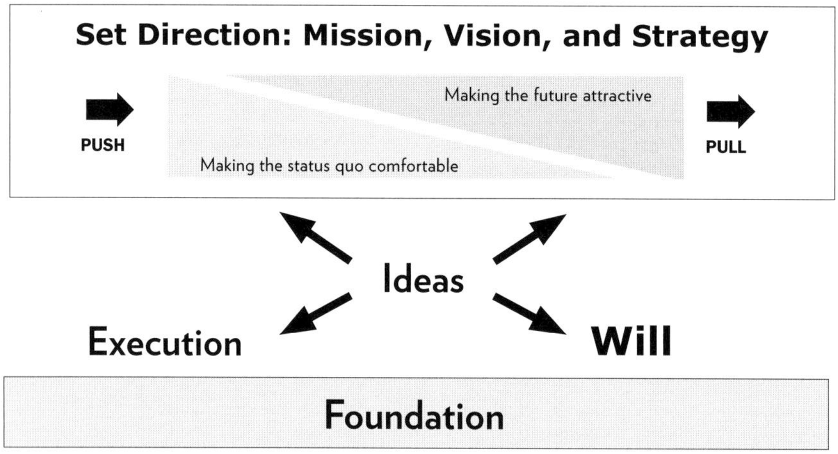

From Seven Leadership Leverage Points for Organization-Level Improvement in Health Care *(2nd Edition), by J. L. Reinertsen, M. Bisognano, and M. D. Pugh, Cambridge, MA: Institute for Healthcare Improvement. Copyright 2008. Reprinted with permission.*

Figure 6. Detailed Framework for Leadership for Improvement

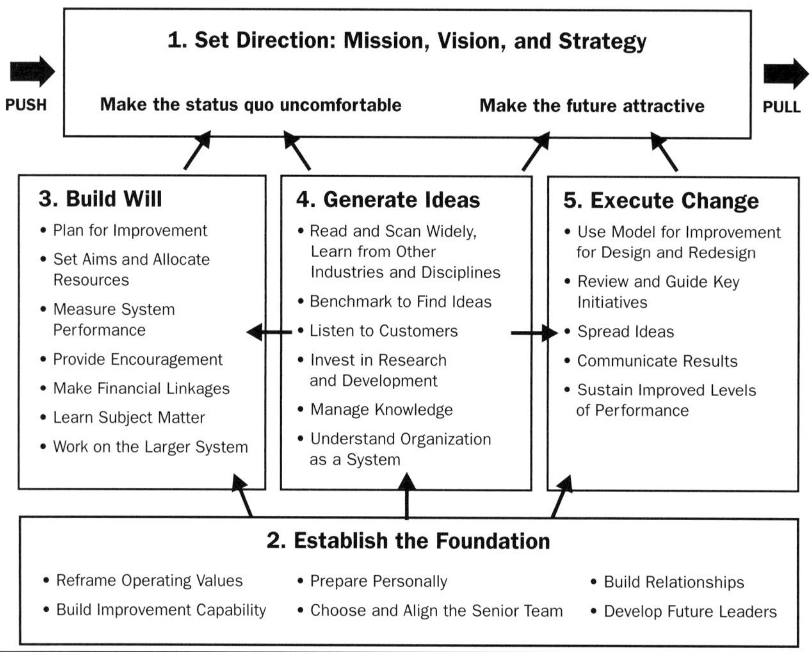

From Seven Leadership Leverage Points for Organization-Level Improvement in Health Care *(2nd Edition), by J. L. Reinertsen, M. Bisognano, and M. D. Pugh, Cambridge, MA: Institute for Healthcare Improvement. Copyright 2008. Reprinted with permission.*

Figure 7. Leadership Framework as an Integrated System

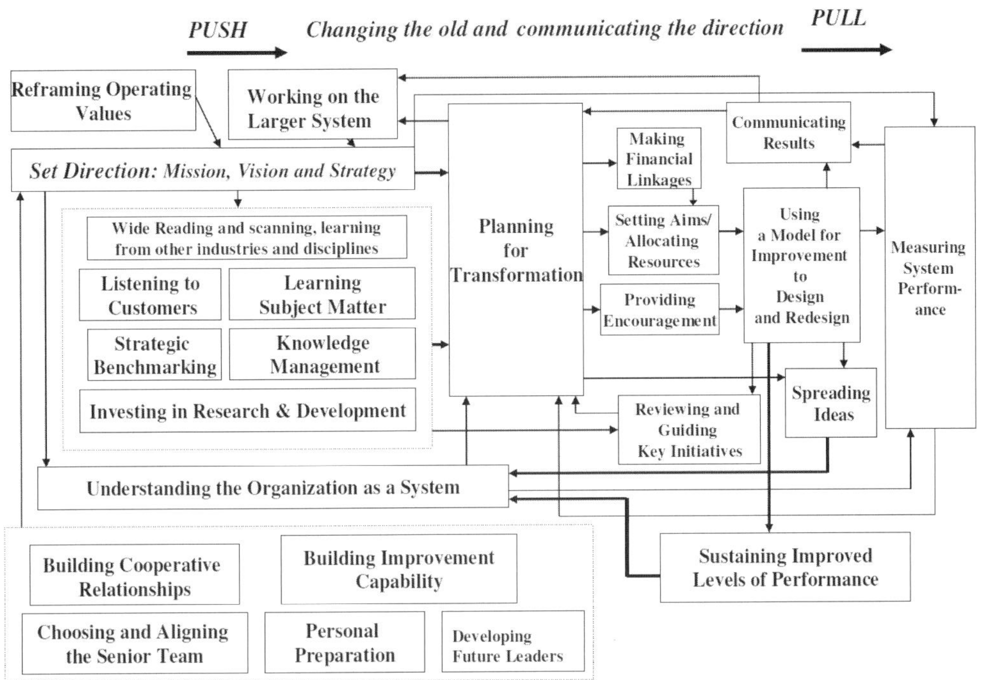

From "Building a System of Leadership for Improvement," in A Framework for Leadership of Improvement *(p. 4), by Institute for Healthcare Improvement, February 2006, Cambridge, MA: IHI. Available at www.knowledge.scot.nhs.uk/media/CLT/ResourceUploads/4012931/IHILeadershipFramework_FEB2006versionFINAL.pdf. Reprinted with permission.*

Figure 8. Cascading Series of Goals and Drivers

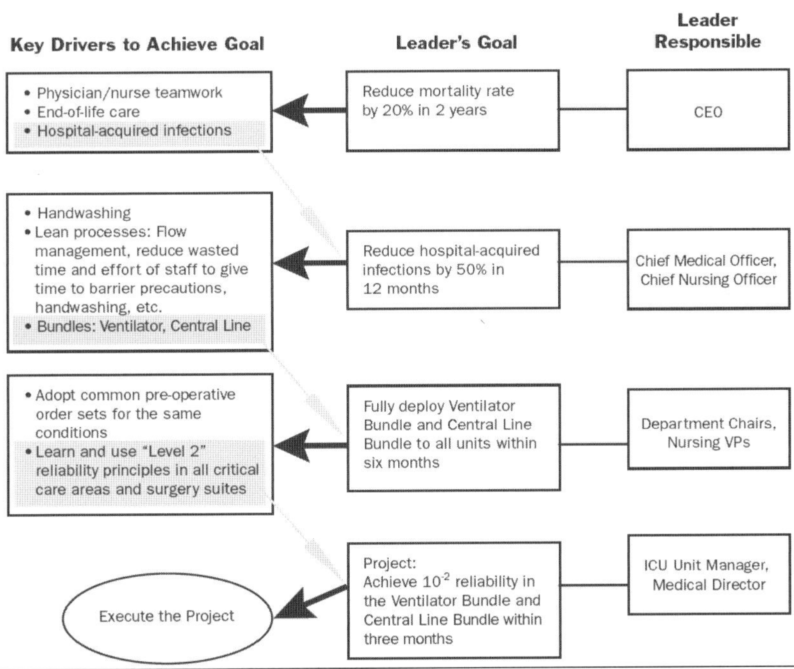

From Seven Leadership Leverage Points for Organization-Level Improvement in Health Care *(2nd Edition, p. 14), by J. L. Reinertsen, M. Bisognano, and M. D. Pugh, Cambridge, MA: Institute for Healthcare Improvement. Reprinted with permission.*

high-risk processes, high-risk patients and populations, high-risk medications, or high-risk actions or interventions. The level of risk is based on the potential consequences of injury or harm to patients. Another aspect in assessing level of risk is the frequency with which the process or procedure is performed. For example, responding to a case of malignant hyperthermia would be considered high risk for the patient, and if the staff does not manage this scenario often, they may not respond as a highly effective team. Therefore, it may be a priority to perform drills to ensure that staff is competent. Managing high-risk patients and processes will significantly affect morbidity and mortality. Examples of high-risk processes include

- core processes: admission, transfer, discharge;
- high-risk processes: medication delivery or administration, surgery, resuscitation;
- high-risk patients: patients with reduced renal function, immunocompromised patients, neonates, patients in critical care units, suicidal patients, dementia patients at risk for wandering;
- high-risk medications: heparin (and oral anticoagulants), insulin, chemotherapy, opiates, neuromuscular blocking agents; and
- high-risk actions and interventions: blood transfusions, use of restraints, extracorporeal circulation, moderate sedation (White, 2004).

After priorities are established, specific initiatives or activities are undertaken. Key steps to implementing PI activities are as follows (Rosati, 2003; White, 2004). These steps ensure success of the PI priorities:

1. Ensure leadership support and commitment for the PI initiative.
2. Assess priority and feasibility of initiative based on risk, resources, leadership support, and organizational strategies.
3. Identify the aim of the initiative and include the topic, process, or problem to be improved (have a good rationale).
4. Convene an interdisciplinary team of content and process experts with all key disciplines as participants (involve all the right stakeholders and have a champion for the change).
5. Use tools and techniques to analyze processes, best practices, research, and consensus-based evidence for the desired change.
6. Develop the change to be implemented and add timelines and accountability for the project.
7. Identify the measures to demonstrate that the change has resulted in improvement; set performance goals.
8. Educate staff on the desired change.
9. Implement and test the change via the redesigned processes.
10. Collect, analyze, and evaluate data on the redesigned process.
11. Make additional changes based on findings and disseminate to all areas.
12. Report and display results to reward staff for improvements.
13. Continue to monitor performance to ensure that the change is sustained.
14. Compare performance internally and externally.
15. Celebrate successes internally and externally.

When choosing between improvement activities, use a prioritization matrix (**Figure 9**) to assist in evaluating the items against specific criteria. After leaders determine the improvement priorities for process improvement, they make decisions about the need to organize a team. A prioritization matrix organizes tasks, issues, or actions and prioritizes them based on agreed-upon criteria. The tool is helpful in identifying criteria for specific priorities and applying a rating scale to help make decisions for the selection of specific activities. This matrix applies options under discussion to the priority considerations of the organization. The tool combines the tree diagram and the L-shaped matrix diagram, displaying the best possible effect. The prioritization matrix is often used before more complex matrices are needed. This matrix applies options under discussion to the priority considerations of the organization.

A project selection matrix ranks and compares potential project areas for implementation. Ranking criteria may include organizational and strategic goals, potential financial impact to the organization, effect on patient and employee satisfaction, likelihood of success, and completion within a specified time frame.

1. Reengineering or System Redesign

In the 1990s, reengineering was one of the major initiatives in hospitals. Most of these efforts were focused on workforce redesign. There was typically a focus on restructuring or redesigning systems and departments into more efficient processes. For example, hospitals experimented with creating new positions that combined work from several different areas. A focus on cross-functional capabilities led to the dissolution of departmental silos. A "patient service associate" or "technical associate" would deliver meals, clean patient rooms, stock supplies, and provide patient transportation. Many hospitals thought that reengineering would increase profit margins and create financial stability. The problem was that reengineering often became associated with downsizing and layoffs. When this happened, employee morale declined and productivity suffered. Because of these negative connotations, reengineering has fallen out of vogue and been replaced by other improvement models and initiatives. The newer approach is to consider adopting the Lean Enterprise method to increase financial stability by eliminating waste.

The key components and tools of a Lean Enterprise include identifying value (value stream mapping and voice of customer), eliminating waste (**Table 5**), establishing flow, enabling pull (instead of push) systems, and pursuing perfection. The Six Sigma method includes a five-step process: define, measure, analyze, improve, and control (DMAIC). Lean Enterprise and Six

Figure 9. Prioritization Matrix: Clinical Improvement Priorities

	High Risk	High Volume	Problem Prone	Cost	Customer Satisfaction	Regulatory	Total
Infection Rates	3	2	2	3	1	3	14
Surgical Complications	2	1	2	3	1	3	12
Emergency Department Time to Treatment	1	3	1	1	3	0	9
Falls With Injuries	2	1	1	2	2	2	10
Medication Safety	3	3	3	2	1	2	14

How to construct

1. Create an L-shaped matrix.
2. Prioritize and assign weights to the list of criteria that will be used in the prioritization.
3. Prioritize the list of options based on each criterion.
4. Prioritize and select the items across all the criteria.

When to use

When problem are identified and options must be narrowed down, when options have strong interrelationships, and when options all need to be done but prioritization or sequencing is needed

Table 5. Types of Waste in Lean Production Systems

Type of Waste	Waste Description	Lean Strategy to Eliminate Waste
Transportation	Moving material or information	One-piece flow, avoid batching
Inventory (overproduction)	Having more material than you need	Standard work, 5-S tool
Motion	Moving people to access or process material or information	Quick changeover, work cell, standard work
Waiting	People waiting for material or information, or material or information waiting to be processed	Quick changeover, one-piece flow, avoid batching
Overproduction	Creating too much material or information	Standard work, one-piece flow, avoid batching
Overprocessing	Processing more than necessary to achieve the desired output	Mistake-proofing, standard work
Defects (necessitating rework)	Errors or mistakes necessitating rework to correct the problem	Mistake-proofing, standard work

Sigma are often complementary tools. Lean Enterprise focuses on dramatically improving flow in the value stream and eliminating waste to improve efficiency and speed. Six Sigma focuses on eliminating defects and reducing variation in processes to improve effectiveness.

Berwick and Hackbarth (2012) believe that the best healthcare reform and cost reduction strategy is to eliminate waste. They have identified six categories where considerable costs are represented by waste. Below is a list of categories and the estimated wasteful spending to the U.S. healthcare system. Total waste detailed below cost the United States $558 billion–$1,263 billion in 2011.

1. Failures of care delivery: waste from poor execution or lack of best practice adoption resulting in injuries and poor outcomes ($102 billion–$154 billion)
2. Failures of care coordination: waste related to fragmented care resulting in complications, readmissions, declines in functional status, and increased dependency of the chronically ill ($25 billion–$45 billion)
3. Overtreatment: waste from rendering care that is not useful ($158 billion–$226 billion)
4. Administrative complexity: waste from state and federal government, accrediting agencies, and payers creating inefficient or misguided rules ($107 billion–$389 billion)
5. Pricing failures: waste related to overpriced procedures and professional fees ($84 billion–$178 billion)
6. Fraud and abuse: waste from fraudsters and fake healthcare bills ($82 billion–$272 billion; pp. E1-E2)

H. Facilitate Development of QPI Action Plans and Projects

Once QPI priorities have been identified, an action plan puts them into motion. A standard format includes

- who (accountability),
- what (specific actions or steps to be followed),
- when (time frame),
- status (progress made and ongoing monitoring), and
- completion (closure or closing the loop).

Projects vary greatly, ranging from improving a defined process to complete redesign or even designing a new process or system. Although the scope varies, the key format remains constant. The level of detail, number of steps, and length of time to complete will vary greatly. **Figure 10** shows the framework for execution of plans for a QPI project (Nolan, 2007, p. 5).

I. Facilitate Program Development Evaluation Planning, Projects, and Activities

Healthcare quality professionals often guide the planning and evaluation for projects and activities. The first step is to understand data and tools to construct an overall plan and specifically the data collection plan. This will include the following steps:

- Determine who, what, when, where, how, and why.
- Structure the design.
- Choose and develop a sampling method.
- Determine and conduct training.
- Delegate responsibilities.
- Facilitate coordination.
- Forecast budget.
- Conduct pilots or tests of change.

A clear understanding of data and tools to assist in problem identification and solutions is needed to facilitate planning and evaluating improvement projects. An overview of data and data management is provided with some of the more common tools used in these processes.

1. Decision-Making Methods and Tools

Described next are QPI methods and tools for decision making, measuring variation, and process improvement. Detailed descriptions and examples of these tools follow. More tools on data analysis and statistical process control are described in *Q Solutions: Information Management*.

Figure 10. Framework for Execution

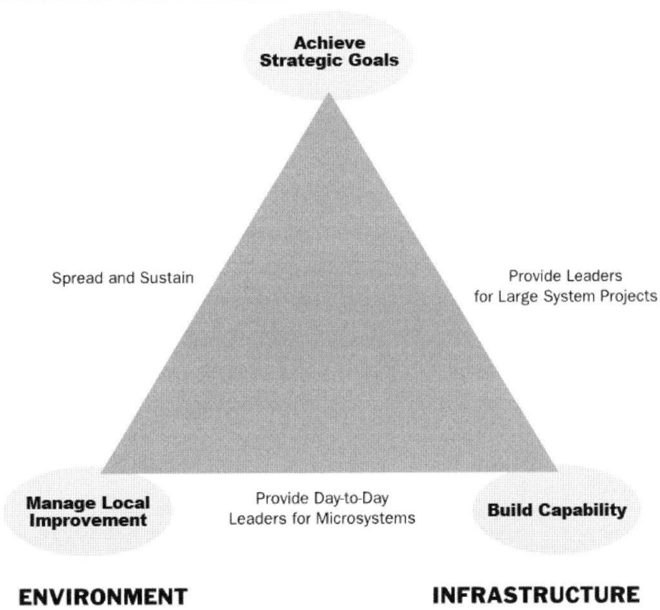

From Seven Leadership Leverage Points for Organization-Level Improvement in Health Care *(2nd Edition, p. 5), by J. L. Reinertsen, M. Bisognano, and M. D. Pugh, Cambridge, MA: Institute for Healthcare Improvement. Copyright 2008. Reprinted with permission.*

Brainstorming (Figure 11). *Brainstorming* is a free-flowing generation of ideas. This approach has the potential to generate excitement, equalize involvement, and result in original solutions to the problem. There is no censoring or discussion of ideas as they are generated, but the team can build upon the ideas of others. It is very important that no judgments are made concerning the idea's worth to the process, or whether the idea is even feasible (money is no object in a brainstorming exercise). Discussion of ideas comes at a later point in the process. This technique works well to generate ideas for tools including the cause-and-effect diagram and the tree diagram.

Multivoting (Figure 12). *Multivoting* is an easy, quick method for determining the most popular or important items from a list. The method uses a series of votes to cut the list in half each time, thus reducing the number of items to be considered.

Nominal group technique (Figure 13). This is a group decision-making process for generating a large number of ideas in which each member works by himself or herself. This technique is used when group members are new to each other or when they have different opinions and goals. This approach is more structured than brainstorming and multivoting.

Delphi Method. The *Delphi method* is a combination of the brainstorming, multivoting, and nominal group techniques. This technique is used when group members are not in one location and often is conducted by e-mail when a meeting is not feasible. After each step in

Figure 11. Brainstorming

How to construct

1. Define the brainstorming topic.
2. Inform participants of the ground rules that (a) "all ideas are good ideas" and (b) "all comments/evaluation should be held in abeyance until the brainstorming is complete."
3. Give everyone a few minutes to think about the topic and write down their ideas.
4. Have the team members call out their ideas. This can be free-flowing, or a structure can be used, such as going around the table with each person verbalizing one idea each time around.
5. As the ideas are generated, one person should write the ideas on a flip chart.

When to use

- Use when a list of possible ideas is needed.
- This technique works well to generate ideas for such tools as the cause-and-effect diagram and the tree diagram.

Figure 12. Multivoting

How to construct

1. Generate a list of items and number them.
2. If the group agrees, combine items that seem to be similar.
3. If necessary, renumber all items.
4. Each member lists on a sheet of paper the items he or she considers the most important (the number of items chosen should be at least one-third of the total number of items on the list).
5. Tally the votes beside each item on the list.
6. Eliminate items with the lowest scores.
7. Repeat the above process until the list is narrowed down to an appropriate number for the group to focus on or the item with the top priority is identified.

When to use

Use after a brainstorming session to identify the key items on which the group will focus.

the process, the data are sent to one person, who compiles the data and sends out the next round for participants to complete.

Failure Mode and Effects Analysis (FMEA). FMEA is a preventive approach to identify failures and opportunities for error and can be used for processes as well as equipment. The traditional techniques for FMEA originated in manufacturing and other industries and have been adapted to healthcare. The Veterans Affairs National Center for Patient Safety created the Healthcare FMEA™ (HFMEA) specifically for healthcare. There are six main steps to HFMEA, as displayed in **Figure 14**.

Prioritization Matrix (Figure 15). This tool organizes tasks, issues, or actions and prioritizes them based on agreed-upon criteria. The tool combines the tree diagram and the L-shaped matrix diagram, displaying the best possible effect. The prioritization matrix often is used before more complex matrices are needed. This matrix applies options under discussion to the priority considerations of the organization.

Figure 13. Nominal Group Technique

How to construct

1. Define the task as you would for brainstorming.
2. Describe the purpose of this technique and the process to the group.
3. Write the question to be answered for all to see. Be sure to clarify the question as needed for the group.
4. Generate ideas to address the identified question by having the group write down their ideas in silence.
5. List all the items as you would in brainstorming, only be sure to use a structured approach so that all ideas are listed (again, there is to be no discussion of the items at this time).
6. Clarify and discuss the ideas one at a time.
7. Give each member 4–8 cards or pieces of paper.
8. Members write one selection from the list on each card and assign a point value to each item. The highest value should be assigned to the most important item (i.e., if there are four cards, the most important card is numbered 4, next important 3, etc.)
9. The cards are collected and the votes are tallied; mark each item on the list with the value on the cards for that item.
10. The item with the largest number becomes the group's selection/priority.

When to use

- Use when team members are new to each other.
- Use when dealing with a controversial topic.

Figure 14. Healthcare Failure Mode and Effects Analysis (HFMEA)

How to construct

There are six main steps to HFMEA℠:

1. Define a topic and process to be studied.
2. Convene an interdisciplinary team with content and process experts.
3. Develop a flow diagram of the process with consecutive numbering of each step and lettering of all subprocesses.
4. List all possible failure modes of each subprocess, including the severity and probability of the failure mode, and then number these failure modes (brainstorming may be helpful to identify failure modes).
5. After analyzing the failure modes, determine the action for each failure mode to eliminate, control, or accept.
6. Identify the corresponding outcome measure to test the redesigned process (White, 2004, p. 61).

Figure 15. Prioritization Matrix: Decision Example

	Low Cost	High Strategic Priority	Meets Accreditation Standards	MD Concern	Staff Concern	Totals
Repair roof	3	4	2	3	4	16
Purchase new X-ray machine	5	2	0	1	5	13
Develop skilled nursing	4	1	0	2	2	9
Develop better communications with home health	2	3	1	4	3	13
Develop staff newsletter	1	5	3	5	1	15

How to construct

1. Create a L-shaped matrix.
2. Prioritize and assign weights to the list of criteria that will be used in the prioritization.
3. Prioritize the list of options based on each criterion.
4. Prioritize and select the item(s) across all of the criteria.

When to use

- When issues are identified and options must be narrowed down
- When options have strong interrelationships
- When options all need to be done, but prioritization or sequencing is needed.

Determining the cause of variation is critical in the QPI process.

Common-Cause Variation. Variation is inherent in any process. On a control chart, this type of variation is exhibited as points between the control limits in no particular pattern. This is variation that normally would be expected from a process. If this type of variation is treated as being unpredictable, it could interfere with the process and make things worse. The root cause of the variation must be identified before any attempt is made to fix the problem.

Special-Cause Variation. Variation that arises from sources that are not inherent in the process is unpredictable. On a control chart, this type of variation is exhibited as points that fall outside the control limits or, when inside the control limits, exhibit certain patterns. These special-cause variations should be addressed whenever they occur, with interventions appropriate for the elimination of the special cause, if possible.

Root-Cause Analysis. When variation is inherent in the process and a reduction of the variation is desired, the root cause of the variation must be identified to eliminate tampering with the effective components of the process. The Joint Commission requires this in response to sentinel events. To start with, potential causes of the variation should be identified. An interdisciplinary team very familiar with the process should use brainstorming, flowcharting, cause-and-effect diagrams, or some other process to determine these potential causes. The second step is to verify the potential causes by collecting data about the process. After the data are collected and analyzed using the tools discussed in this module, the actual causes of the variation (or at least the most probable causes) can be identified. The following areas should be addressed in the analysis:

- human factors: communications and information management systems;
- human factors: training;
- human factors: fatigue and scheduling;
- environmental factors;
- equipment factors;

- rules, policies, and procedures; and
- leadership systems and culture (White, 2004).

At this point, the team should develop and implement an action plan designed to eliminate or minimize the root causes of the variation.

Spaghetti Diagram (Figure 16). A *spaghetti diagram*, also called a layout diagram, is a graphic representation of the flow of traffic or movement.

Checklist (Figure 17). A *checklist* is a standard way to ensure completion of critical tasks for a process or activity.

5-S (Figure 18). 5-S is a lean tool that represents Sort, Straighten, Scrub/Shine, Systematize/Sustain, Standardize.

Value Stream Mapping (Figure 19). *Value stream mapping* is a map of the process in which only value-added steps for the customer are retained and other waste removed.

Voice of the Customer (Figure 20). *Voice of the Customer* is a list of needs, wants, and desires of the customer of a process output. These are sometimes called specifications or requirements.

Supplier Input Process Output Customer (SIPOC; Figure 21). A SIPOC is a tool in process management to identify key drivers of a process.

When the healthcare quality professional has a clear understanding of data, types of data, and tools, the process steps may be described with a variety of acronyms (e.g., Plan-Do-Study-Act [PDSA]; Plan-Do-Check-Act [PDCA]; assess, plan, implement, evaluate [APIE]) but include the similar components. For this module no specific improvement model is endorsed so that the healthcare quality professional can use tools depending on the improvement question and the organizational context. Regardless of the improvement model, the improvement process seeks to accomplish the following:

- Ensure the project is a priority for the organization and is aligned with the strategic plan.
- Ensure leadership support and commitment.
- Assess the priority and feasibility of initiatives based on risks, resources, leadership support, and organizational strategies.
- Clarify the aim, stated in specific measurable terms.
- Present baseline data analysis that illustrates the problem. Use tools and techniques to analyze.
- Demonstrate that the aim is based on own data and identifies the specific problem to be solved, the program to be enhanced, or the process or system to be redesigned.
- Select an interdisciplinary team with content and process experts and all key disciplines as members.
- Map the current process and collect data on key aspects of the process. Continue to use data and tools to identify bottlenecks, constraints, delays, and other barriers.
- Define measures and collect data. Indicate how you will know a change is an improvement.
- Describe the change to be made.
- Implement the change (small tests of change or pilot tests).
- Study the effects of the change and make a decision: adopt, adapt, or abandon the specific change.
- Map the new process.
- Spread the change throughout the organization in a defined implementation plan (include communication plan and education plan).
- Sustain the improvement by monitoring.

Figure 16. Spaghetti Diagram (or Layout Diagram)

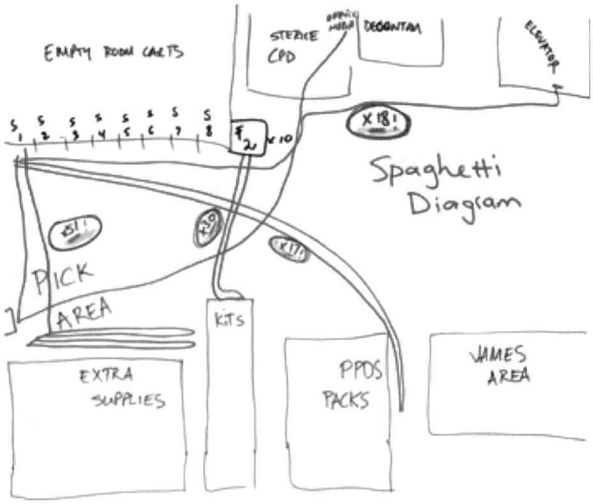

How to construct

1. Get a layout or blueprint of the area.
2. Pick the subject to follow for the flow.
3. Record every movement until completed.

When to use

- To demonstrate flow or movement in a process
- To identify excess or wasted travel or movement

Figure 17. Checklist

Completion	Task

How to construct

1. Identify critical elements or tasks to be completed for a process.
2. Make a list of all elements with a space to indicate completion of the task before moving to the next item.

When to use

- When reliance on memory is not sufficient
- When tasks for a process or activity are critical and omission may cause harm

Figure 18. 5-S

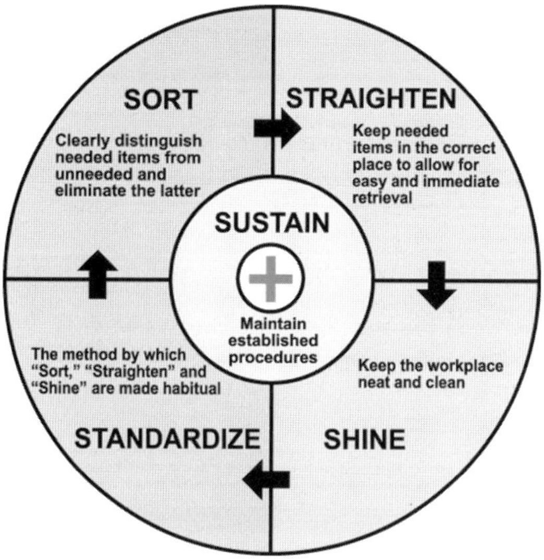

How to construct

1. Use the five components to divide all items into categories (retain, return, rid).
2. Find a place for everything and put everything in place.
3. Clean the entire area.
4. Establish schedules and systems to maintain the area.
5. Form a new habit to sustain the performance.

When to use

- To establish orderly flow, eliminate waste, and organize the workplace
- To standardize the work setting

From "Lean Manufacturing and Environment", by the U.S. Environmental Protection Agency, November 10, 2011. Available at http://www.epa.gov/lean/environment/methods/fives.htm.

J. Selection of Process and Outcome Measures

There are several types of performance measures. Before selecting a measure, one must understand what purpose each measure serves.

- Structural measures are measures of infrastructure, capacity, systems, and processes (e.g., nurse staffing ratios).
- Process measures are measures of process performance. They tell whether the parts or steps in the system are performing as planned. This can be "in process" or "end of process" (e.g., timely administration of prophylactic surgical antibiotics).
- Outcome measures are results of overall process or system performance (often risk adjusted; e.g., mortality).
- Balancing measures are measures that tell us what happened to the system as the process or outcome measures improved. They may be the consequence of or affected by another measure. The term *unintended consequence* is another way of thinking about balancing measures. For example, if the organization is working to reduce cesarean section (C-section) rates, a balancing measure to ensure that the change in C-section rates does

Figure 19. Value Stream Mapping

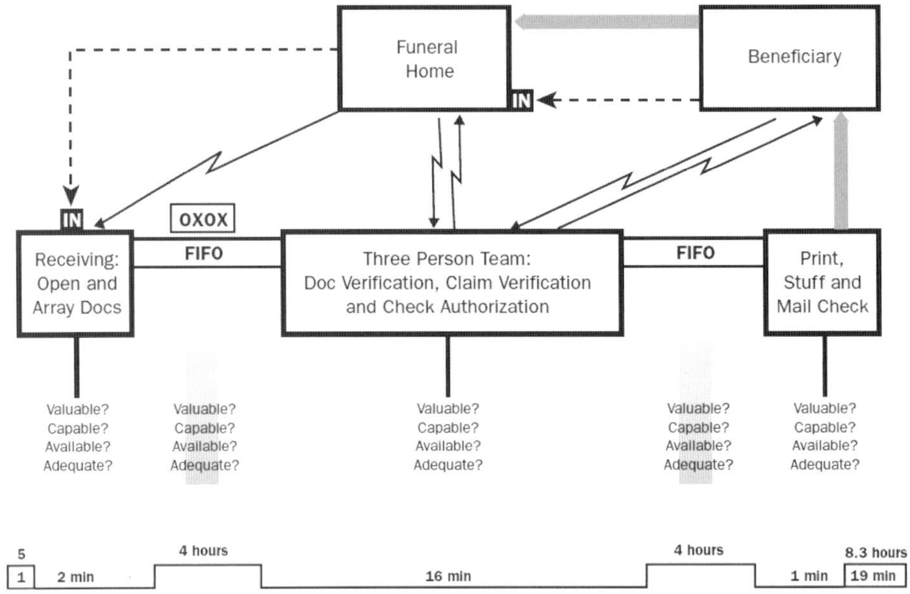

How to construct

1. Identify the current process (mark steps that are of no value to the customer or required by some regulatory body).
2. Identify the ideal process state.
3. Close the gap between the two states.

When to use

To improve flow of the process, reduce waste, and implement lean functioning

From Going Lean in Health Care *(p. 8), by the Institute for Healthcare Improvement, 2005, Cambridge, MA: IHI. Reprinted with permission.*

Figure 20. Voice of the Customer

- What do you like about the current process?
- What do you think needs improvement?
- What would you recommend to improve the current process?
- What could threaten the success of the project?

How to construct

1. Identify customers of a process output.
2. Develop a list of questions to ask customers about the process and their needs.
3. Refine the list to use with the process review and improvement.

When to use

To improve a process

Figure 21. Supplier Input Process Output Customer (SIPOC)

S	I	P	O	C
Supplier name	Process input	Process step 1	Process output	Customer name
Supplier name	Process input	Process step 2	Process output	Customer name
Supplier name	Process input	Process step 3	Process output	Customer name

How to construct

1. Identify each element of the SIPOC and list across the top of a page.
2. Under each heading of SIPOC list the suppliers, their inputs, the process, the customers, and the outputs.

When to use

To identify internal and external customer needs in a process and to use with other lean tools for process improvement

not have a negative consequence is to monitor maternal and infant morbidity and mortality. The balancing measures of maternal and infant morbidity and mortality could be affected if a needed C-section is delayed trying to increase vaginal deliveries and reduce C-sections.

Numerous measures have been developed, vetted, and put into widespread use. Healthcare quality professionals should not develop their own measures because there are a multitude of valid and reliable measures that have been evaluated and endorsed by various public-private partnerships (i.e., NQF) and professional associations. The sources of these measures generally include the following:

- administrative data (volumes, admissions, discharges, length of stay, billing data, codes, Uniform Hospital Discharge Data Set [UHDDS]),
- patient medical records (clinical care, medication use, surgery and procedural data, treatment data),
- standardized clinical data sets (core measures, ORYX®, minimum data set [MDS], Outcome and Assessment Information Set [OASIS], National Surgical Quality Improvement Program [NSQIP], Healthcare Effectiveness Data and Information Set [HEDIS], Agency for Healthcare Research and Quality [AHRQ] Quality Indicators [Inpatient Quality Indicators, Patient Safety Indicators, Pediatric Quality Indicators, Leapfrog Group's Measures, National Hospital Quality Measures]),
- patient surveys (Consumer Assessment of Healthcare Providers and Systems [CAHPS]),
- employee patient safety culture surveys, and
- comments from individual patients and their families (complaint management).

The AHRQ has been instrumental in advancing the study of measures, especially outcomes and the effectiveness of specific treatments. Criteria have been developed for the selection of measures based on attributes (AHRQ, 2012) that include the following:

- Standardization: Reporting the same kind of data in the same way;
- Comparability: If appropriate, results are risk adjusted for factors (e.g., age, gender, health status);
- Availability: Data will be available;
- Timeliness: Results will be available when most needed;

- Relevance: Results measure concerns of stakeholders and users;
- Validity: Measures have been tested so they consistently and accurately reflect the measure;
- Experience: Organizations have experience with the measure so it reflects actual performance;
- Stability: The measure is not likely to be removed from use;
- Evaluability: The measure can be evaluated as better or worse;
- Distinguishability: The measure denotes differences between organizations;
- Credibility: The measures can be audited.

Another important resource for measures and measure sets is the National Quality Forum (NQF, 2011). **Table 6** identifies the NQF measure evaluation evidence criteria to support the focus of measurement.

When measures have been developed or selected for use, there must be a context in which to determine whether the performance of a specific measure is good. In order to determine the goodness, there are several factors to consider. First, does the evidence preestablish the desired or expected performance level? If not, does any regulatory, accreditation, or payer agencies identify a desired or expected performance level? The use of comparative data will assist the organization in setting desired targets or goals and provide a method by which to determine how well the organization is performing compared with similar organizations, competitors, best in the industry, and best in class.

1. Comparative Data

Healthcare quality professionals facilitate analysis and interpretation of outcomes and decision support data for the organization. The reference point for the outcome data must always be kept in mind whenever the results of such data are analyzed. The overall goals for outcomes and decision support data are to improve quality, reduce costs and resource consumption, increase profitability of the organization, and develop an information-based strategic plan. Comparisons of length of stay, costs, complications, and mortality cannot be made legitimately without adjusting severity at the patient level. Severity adjustment and clinical case mix permit effective analysis and eliminate practitioners' concerns that "their patients are sicker."

Decision support data facilitate cross-functional analyses to improve patient care processes and outcomes. Decision support data integrate financial and clinical data and provide the opportunity to perform highly sophisticated data analysis, involving predictive outcome management. These data help healthcare quality managers and executive staff evaluate current operations and the feasibility of the development of new product lines and services.

Healthcare quality managers coordinate the outcome and decision support data by posing pertinent questions:

- What kinds of comparative analyses will be most important?
- With whom should we compare ourselves?
- How can we be sure the data are really comparable?
- What do we do when the data reveal significant differences in our outcomes and the outcomes of the peer or benchmark?

2. Benchmarking

The healthcare organization's leaders can begin to ask questions internally to determine the cause of variances revealed by comparisons. The challenge for healthcare quality staff is to display the outcome data in a meaningful way that will be used by the involved departments or teams. Graphic display of the data improves understanding and usefulness of the results.

Table 6. Evidence to Support the Focus of Measurement

Type of Measures	Evidence	Example of Measure Type and Evidence to Be Addressed
Health Outcome An outcome of care is the health status of a patient (or change in health status) resulting from healthcare, desirable or adverse. In some situations, resource use may be considered a proxy for a health state (e.g., hospitalization may represent deterioration in health status).	A rationale supports the relationship of the health outcome to at least one healthcare structure, process, intervention, or service.	#0230: Acute myocardial infarction (AMI). 30-day mortality. Survival is a goal of seeking and providing treatment for AMI. Rationale linking healthcare processes or interventions (aspirin, reperfusion) to mortality or survival. #0171: Acute care hospitalization (risk-adjusted) [of home care patients]. Improvement or stabilization of condition to remain at home is a goal of seeking and providing home care services. Rationale linking healthcare processes (e.g., medication reconciliation, care coordination) to hospitalization of patients receiving home care services. #0140: Ventilator-associated pneumonia for intensive care unit (ICU) and high-risk nursery patients. Avoiding harm from treatment is a goal when seeking and providing healthcare. Rationale linking healthcare processes (e.g., ventilator bundle) to ventilator-acquired pneumonia.
Intermediate Clinical Outcome An intermediate outcome is a change in physiologic state that leads to a longer-term health outcome.	Quantity, quality, and consistency of a body of evidence that the measured intermediate clinical outcome leads to a desired health outcome.	#0059: Hemoglobin A1c management (A1c > 9). Evidence that hemoglobin A1c level leads to health outcomes (e.g., prevention of renal disease, heart disease, amputation, mortality).
Process A process of care is a healthcare-related activity performed for, on behalf of, or by a patient.	Quantity, quality, and consistency of a body of evidence that the measured healthcare process leads to desired health outcomes in the target population with benefits that outweigh harms to patients. Specific drugs and devices should have Food and Drug Administration approval for the target condition. If the measure focus is on inappropriate use, then quantity, quality, and consistency of a body of evidence that the measured healthcare process does *not* lead to desired health outcomes in the target population.	#0551: Angiotensin-converting enzyme (ACE) inhibitor and angiotensin receptor blocker (ARB) use and persistence among members with coronary artery disease at high risk for coronary events. Evidence that use of ACE inhibitor and ARB results in lower mortality or cardiac events. #0058: Inappropriate antibiotic treatment for adults with acute bronchitis. Evidence that antibiotics are not effective for acute bronchitis.

(continued)

Table 6. Evidence to Support the Focus of Measurement *(continued)*

Type of Measures	Evidence	Example of Measure Type and Evidence to Be Addressed
Structure Structure of care is a feature of a healthcare organization or clinician related to its capacity to provide high-quality healthcare.	Quantity, quality, and consistency of a body of evidence that the measured healthcare structure leads to desired health outcomes with benefits that outweigh harms (including evidence of the link to effective care processes and the link from the care processes to desired health outcomes).	#0190: Nurse staffing hours. Evidence that increasing nursing hours results in lower mortality or morbidity or leads to provision of effective care processes (e.g., lower medication errors) that lead to better outcomes.
Special Considerations by Topic		
Patient Experience with Care	Evidence that the measured aspects of care are those valued by patients and for which the patient is the best or only source of information (often acquired through qualitative studies) *or* Evidence that patient experience with care is correlated with desired outcomes.	#0166: HCAHPS. Evidence that patients or consumers value the aspects of care being measured (e.g., communication with doctors and nurses, responsiveness of hospital staff, pain control, communication about medicines, cleanliness and quiet of the hospital environment, and discharge information).
Efficiency Measures of efficiency combine the concepts of resource use and quality.	Efficiency measured with combination of quality measures and resource-use measures. Quality measure component: Evidence for the selected quality measures as described in this table. Resource-use measure component: Does not require clinical evidence as described in this table.	Currently, there are no NQF-endorsed efficiency measures that combine quality and resource use. Potential measure: Diabetes quality measures or composite used in conjunction with a measure of resource use per episode. Evidence for diabetes quality measures as described in this table.

From Guidance for Evaluating the Evidence Related to the Focus of Quality Measurement and Importance to Measure and Report *(p. 15–16), by the National Quality Forum, January 2011, Washington, DC: NQF. Available at www.qualityforum.org/WorkArea/linkit.aspx?LinkIdentifier=id&ItemID=70941. Reprinted with permission.*

Benchmarking is the comparison of an organization's or an individual practitioner's results against a reference point. Ideally, the reference point should be a demonstrated best practice. Healthcare quality professionals assist the organization and its practitioners in interpreting benchmarking results. It is important to clarify two very important aspects of benchmarking. The organization's or practitioner's actual performance or outcomes always stay the same. However, depending on to whom the organization or physician is compared, the expected value can change. For instance, an organization's complication rate may only be 6% higher than expected when compared with a selected market. However, the same organization may have an 11% higher-than-expected complication rate when compared with the U.S. average. In other words, the comparison value and the magnitude of difference change.

Healthcare quality professionals need to ask the right questions to find out how their organization works and then ask more questions to compare it with the best performers. The goal is to identify how to improve the organization's outcomes, not to identify the differences between it and the benchmarking partner. It is important to be able to take the benchmarking data and provide the pertinent results to the right audience. When variance is identified, the department or service involved must ask the following questions:

- What are we doing?
- How are we doing it?
- What is the measure of how well we do it?
- Why are we looking for improvement?

Directed and focused questions help managers identify performance gaps. Benchmarking must be an essential element of clinical pathway development to ensure that the highest-cost, highest-opportunity diagnosis-related groups (DRGs) are prioritized. Data-driven internal and external comparisons not only help to set best practices but also appeal to healthcare professionals by providing objective data for clinical pathway development. In general, three steps must be followed in benchmarking clinical pathways:

1. Identify high-resource-use DRGs.
2. Assess internal variability.
3. Benchmark against external sources.

Table 7 provides examples of benchmarking projects.

Benchmarking enables an organization to set a target or goal for its performance improvement activities. It is up to the QPI team to determine whether it wants to be average (the industry standard) or to raise the bar to a much higher level of performance. The goal is to improve performance, so the goal depends on the level of current performance and the commitment of the performance team and healthcare providers. One of the most critical decisions an organization makes when launching a benchmarking initiative is selecting the source of its benchmarking comparative data. Healthcare quality professionals often coordinate an organization's benchmarking efforts. Most healthcare regulatory agencies require benchmarking as part of a comprehensive QPI program.

Potential data sources for benchmarking include the following:

- Government data available from Centers for Medicare & Medicaid Services (CMS) and state government agencies.
- Alliances such as large healthcare systems (partnership organizations often provide data extrapolation for their members, often providing databases for internal and external benchmarking).

Table 7. Examples of Benchmarking Projects

Type of Benchmarking	Example Topic	Measures
Internal	Cesarean section rate	Physician A vs. B vs. C, etc.; physician group practice A vs. B, etc.; physicians vs. midwives.
Internal	Time to antibiotic for XYZ Infection	Emergency department vs. unit A vs. unit B, etc.; emergency department vs. urgent care setting.
External	Use of angiotensin-converting enzyme inhibitors with acute myocardial infarction	Health system or proprietary database performance of all hospitals vs. region vs. similar-size hospital vs. own hospital.
External	Central line–associated bloodstream infection rates	Own unit vs. National Healthcare Safety Network data for similar units. Can compare by quartile or median rates (industry standard).
Zero-incidence	Wrong site, wrong procedure, or wrong person surgery	Own hospital's incidence vs. zero incidence.

- Proprietary databases such as the National Database of Nursing Quality Indicators® (NDNQI®).
- State peer review organizations and state hospital associations that offer free benchmarking opportunities for hospitals in their state.
- For-profit database companies that offer software that helps hospitals or organizations extrapolate and compile their own benchmark data or provide benchmarking data through a centralized database compiled by the company. These data also are reported to regulatory agencies upon request, such as the Joint Commission's ORYX and Core Measures, CMS's OASIS, and the National Committee for Quality Assurance's HEDIS requirement.

V. Decision Support, Risk Adjustment, Data Interpretation, and Benchmarking

A. Decision Support

Performance outcome measurement or decision support systems can provide a primary focus to determine the quality of healthcare services provided to consumers. By analyzing data and information generated by an effective performance outcome measurement system, healthcare quality professionals will be able to help identify areas for improving quality and resources in their organizations. Other uses for outcome systems include helping identify how an organization measures up in relation to its competitors, identifying individual providers and practitioners who meet acceptable levels of quality, allowing providers to respond more rapidly to market changes, and paying for exceptional performance.

Organizations should use available decision support systems to develop an outcome information management plan, which includes evaluating performance outcome measurement systems. Outcomes are viewed in terms of various clinical topics, including mortality, complication rates, infection rates, cesarean section rates, and other clinical outcome measurement categories. Categories might or might not reflect the resources (e.g., cost, charges, length of stay) associated with a given outcome.

To analyze and interpret such outcome data, healthcare quality professionals would start with the type of system. There are two types: electronic health record (EHR)-based and code-based. With EHR-based systems, nursing or medical record analysts review the medical records of all discharged inpatients to capture and input diagnostic, procedural, and detailed clinical findings, such as laboratory results. This is done to identify severity- and risk-adjusted information at the time of the patient's admission and at different points throughout the hospitalization.

Code-based systems are based on retrospective administrative data, such as data in the Uniform Bill document 1992 (UB-92) or claim data. These systems include clinical information spanning the patient's entire stay but not identifying the specific timing of certain conditions. This additional type of information can be available in an EHR-based system. There also are some very significant benefits to using a code-based system, including much lower costs. Another benefit of a code-based system is that is it more likely to contain a sample size sufficient to develop more reliable models and output and to provide sufficient and meaningful groups for comparing data. Most states require hospitals to submit all payer data that are deemed public information. These data can be purchased by an interested organization and then analyzed and interpreted using statistical tools in search of key variables that might predict the likelihood of a desired outcome.

1. Evaluation and Selection of Evidence-Based Practice Guidelines

Evidence-based medicine is the "conscientious, explicit, and judicious use of current best evidence in making decisions about the care of individual patients" (Sackett, Rosenberg, Muir-Gray, Haynes, & Richardson, 1996, p. 71). Because multiple disciplines are involved in healthcare delivery, however, the term *evidence-based practice* (EBP) is more appropriate than evidence-based medicine from a healthcare quality perspective. Clinicians not only should base their care on the experimental evidence but also should consider experiential evidence, physiologic principles, patient and professional values, and system features in their decision making (Tonelli, 2001). This allows individualized application and dissemination of aggregate research evidence (Greenhalgh, 1999; Tonelli, 2001).

EBP promotes patient safety through the provision of effective and efficient healthcare, resulting in less variation in care and fewer unnecessary or nontherapeutic interventions (IOM, 2001). EBP and outcomes measurement are iterative; one facilitates the other (Deaton, 2001). EBP complements the principles of continuous quality improvement (CQI). Outcome evaluation at the individual and aggregate level is an essential step in evaluating the impact of EBP.

Evidence-based quality management is based on two types of research: clinical research and health services research. Clinical research evaluates the impact of interventions on patient outcomes. Outcome measures may include clinical outcomes, functional outcomes, and patient satisfaction. This type of research assists healthcare quality professionals in determining clinical evidence-based best practices. Health services research evaluates the health system at the micro and macro levels. Results from this type of research guide healthcare quality professionals in improving work processes and systems of care.

To facilitate research-based practice—that is, to promote research use—healthcare quality professionals must collaborate with organizational leaders to promote a culture of excellence. Healthcare providers must be motivated to provide the best possible care and to use the best system processes based on the evidence in the research literature or on data obtained in their own organizations. A key strategy is to keep all discussions based on improving the patient's experience and outcomes and keep personality conflicts out of the conversation, based on previously established ground rules. Research use is a key aspect of the CQI process and critical to obtaining healthcare quality as defined by the IOM.

The rating of evidence for EBP is often based on the U.S. Preventive Services Task Force (USPSTF) levels of evidence and grading system. Evidence for practice can be classified according to certain levels or strength of the evidence. The USPSTF has also defined levels of certainty about net benefit. The USPSTF levels of evidence (**Table 8**; Sawaya, Guirguis-Blake, LeFevre, et al., 2007) are often used to rate the evidence so that practitioners can make wise decisions about care and treatment options with some degree of certainty about outcomes. Strong evidence is transformed into practice and then measured in standardized formats. For example, there is strong evidence that timely administration of aspirin in AMI decreases mortality. This practice is then implemented widely, as in the Core Measure for AMI. Organizations operationalize this practice by using clinical pathways, standard order sets, plans of care, and ongoing measurement processes.

Common sources for EBP guidelines and national measures are

- AHRQ (e.g., National Clinical Guideline),
- Cochrane (e.g., clinical evidence comparisons),
- Specialty professional associations and societies (e.g., American Cardiology Association),
- Leapfrog Group (e.g., hospital-based measures), and

Table 8. Levels of Certainty About Net Benefit

Level of Certainty	Description
High	The available evidence usually includes consistent results from well-designed, well-conducted studies in representative primary care populations. These studies assess the effects of the preventive service on health outcomes. This conclusion is therefore unlikely to be strongly affected by the results of future studies.
Moderate	The available evidence is sufficient to determine the effects of the preventive service on health outcomes, but confidence in the estimate is constrained by factors such as • the number, size, or quality of individual studies; • inconsistency of findings across individual studies; • limited generalizability of findings to routine primary care practice; and • lack of coherence in the chain of evidence. As more information becomes available, the magnitude or direction of the observed effect could change, and this change may be large enough to change the conclusion.
Low	The available evidence is insufficient to assess effects on health outcomes. Evidence is insufficient because of • the limited number or size of studies, • important flaws in study design or methods, • inconsistency of findings across individual studies, • gaps in the chain of evidence, • findings not generalizable to routine primary care practice, and • lack of information on important health outcomes. More information may allow estimation of effects on health outcomes.

Note. The USPSTF defines certainty as "likelihood that the USPSTF assessment of the net benefit of a preventive service is correct." The net benefit is defined as benefit minus harm of the preventive service as implemented in a general, primary care population. From "Update on the Methods of the U.S. Preventive Services Task Force: Estimating Certainty and Magnitude of Net Benefit," by G. F. Sawaya, J. Guirguis-Blake, M. LeFevre, and U.S. Preventative Services Task Force, 2007, Annals of Internal Medicine, *147, pp. 871–875. Copyright 2007 by American College of Physicians. Reprinted with permission.*

- NQF (e.g., 29 Never Events, Nurse Sensitive Measures, Ambulatory Sensitive Measures, Long-Term Care Measures, Hospital Measures).

The USPSTF (2008) updated its definitions of the grades it assigns to recommendations and now includes suggestions for practice associated with each grade (**Table 9**). These definitions apply to USPSTF recommendations voted on after May 2007.

2. QPI Research Continuum

QPI activities and research exist on a continuum of rigor, as seen in **Table 10**. Both are based on the scientific method and are used to better understand phenomena. The scientific approach is the most sophisticated method of acquiring knowledge. This approach involves inductive and deductive reasoning to define a process that self-evaluates in an attempt to reach conclusions superior to those arrived at through reliance on tradition, authority, and experience. Integrating the right pieces of data and information into a research-based framework for the study of people was a contribution of the earliest pioneers in the field of healthcare quality.

The underlying assumptions of design, measurement, and interpretation are the same. Healthcare quality professionals should use the level of research rigor that best answers the specific performance improvement question. There needs to be a balance between rigor and practicality (Byers & Beaudin, 2002). Research studies and systematic reviews can be evaluated for usefulness to a practice setting using critical appraisal tools. These tools guide healthcare quality professionals through the research critique process, allowing effective evaluation and synthesis of research findings for use in QPI activities (Byers & Beaudin, 2001).

Table 9. USPSTF Updated Definitions

Grade	Definition	Suggestions for Practice
A	The USPSTF recommends the service. There is high certainty that the net benefit is substantial.	Offer or provide this service.
B	The USPSTF recommends the service. There is high certainty that the net benefit is moderate or there is moderate certainty that the net benefit is moderate to substantial.	Offer or provide this service.
C	*Note: The following statement is undergoing revision.* Clinicians may provide this service to selected patients depending on individual circumstances. However, for most individuals without signs or symptoms, there is likely to be only a small benefit from this service.	Offer or provide this service only if other considerations support offering or providing the service in an individual patient.
D	The USPSTF recommends against the service. There is moderate or high certainty that the service has no net benefit or that the harms outweigh the benefits.	Discourage the use of this service.
I Statement	The USPSTF concludes that the current evidence is insufficient to assess the balance of benefits and harms of the service. Evidence is lacking, of poor quality, or conflicting, and the balance of benefits and harms cannot be determined.	Read the clinical considerations section of USPSTF Recommendation Statement. If the service is offered, patients should understand the uncertainty about the balance of benefits and harms.

From "What the Grades Mean and Suggestions for Practice," by U.S. Preventative Services Task Force, May 2008. Copyright 2008 by USPSTF. Available at www.uspreventiveservicestaskforce.org/uspstf/grades.htm. Reprinted with permission.

Table 10. Research Process Versus Quality Improvement Process

Scientific Process or Research Process	Quality Improvement Process
Identify the information needs or ask the question to be investigated.	Identify the process improvement, survey the literature, and flowchart the process.
Define the variables or the elements for which data are needed.	Define the customers and problem.
Formulate a plan of study or hypotheses.	Formulate a plan.
Choose or design the research design and collection tools or instruments.	Choose one or a combination of basic or quality management and planning tools.
Collect the data.	Collect the data.
Analyze the data.	Analyze the data. Look for root causes.
Display the data.	Display the data.
Report the data and findings.	Report the data and findings.
Draw conclusions.	Draw conclusions.
Act on recommendations deduced from the conclusions.	Act on recommendations deduced from the conclusions.
Continue to monitor the process.	Continue to monitor the process.
Evaluate and communicate conclusions.	Evaluate and communicate conclusions.
	Hold the improvement.

3. Development of Clinical and Critical Pathways or Guidelines

Clinical guidelines are consensus statements developed to assist in clinical management decisions, and clinical pathways are tools to manage quality outcomes and cost of care based on clinical guidelines and current evidence. Clinical pathways are document-based tools that provide a link between the best available evidence and clinical practice. Clinical pathways, also known as care pathways, critical pathways, integrated care pathways, or care maps, are one tool used to manage the quality in healthcare concerning the standardization of care processes. A variety of terms have been used for this tool, and for simplicity the term *clinical pathway* will be used in this module. Clinical pathways support EBP and clinical guidelines in a time-oriented plan. The use of pathways or guidelines reduces variation of clinical practice to optimize patient outcomes. The concept was introduced in 1985 by Karen Zander and Kathleen Bower at the New England Medical Center in Boston. They were early nursing pioneers in applying process management thinking and techniques to improve patient care (Zander & Bower, 1987). Clinical pathways operationalize evidence into daily practice for patient care. Clinical pathways are intended to create an integrated comprehensive approach or plan to the patient's care rather than individual professions functioning independently. Interdisciplinary communication, collaboration, and teamwork are enhanced by working from one pathway, and continuity and care coordination are achieved for the patient.

The pathway shapes expectations or outcomes of care as the patient progresses, based on what is the best practice for most patients most of the time. The pathway is written in a manner to ensure that actions or interventions are completed at designated points with the expected outcome. They are designed to support clinical management, clinical and nonclinical resource management, audit management, and also financial management. Often, the improved clinical outcomes are intended to support cost-effective use of resources such as length of stay, diagnostic tests, and pharmaceutical management. Because there will be differences in patients' responses for the same condition or treatment, individual variances must be captured, documented, and addressed. This continuous monitoring and data evaluation component is essential to pathway improvement through continual revision of pathways. It is expected that over time variation will decrease, costs will decrease, and the value of care will improve.

Although standardization is important to the pathways, they are not intended to be overly prescriptive and should still allow personalized care. However, one critique of pathways is that not all variation in patient care is negative, and standardized care or "cookbook medicine" would be a detriment to patient care and clinician autonomy. Individual patient factors may contribute to variation that cannot or should not be controlled by the system. Pathways tend to address processes in the ideal or uncomplicated patient and may not address problems in the majority of patients. It is important to identify which patients are appropriate for the pathway. In general, pathways are more applicable to patients with uncomplicated illnesses undergoing procedures or surgery. Medical patients may be more difficult to fit into a standard pathway.

The standardized approach is designed to empower patients such that each patient knows the plan and his or her expected outcome at each phase of recovery (e.g., on postoperative day two, the hip replacement patient is expected to ambulate a defined number of steps or feet and void without a urinary catheter). Standardization also helps reduce clinical risk by ensuring that for specific conditions there are no lapses in care to be provided, and if outcomes are not met there is an immediate assessment of the reason. When differences or unwanted variances do occur, they should be noted and accommodations made in the plan of care to ensure safety and effectiveness. Some common areas addressed by clinical pathways include orthopedic surgery such as hips, knees, and shoulders. It should be noted that surgical care is more often conducive to clinical pathways than medical conditions, where more differences in the patient's condition occur.

Clinical pathways facilitate the development of standardized physician order sets, interventions for the patient, and documentation of the patient's condition, and they are often used in the following situations:

- prevalent pathology in the care setting (e.g., pain),
- pathology with a significant risk for patients (e.g., venous thromboembolism),
- pathology with a high cost for the hospital (e.g., total hip joint replacement),
- predictable clinical course (e.g., total knee replacement),
- pathology that is well defined and permits homogeneous care (e.g., laminectomy, transurethral prostate resection),
- existence of recommendations of good practices or experts opinions (e.g., diabetes),
- possibility of obtaining professional agreement (e.g., coronary angioplasty),
- multidisciplinary implementation (e.g., joint replacement), and
- relatively mature guidelines (e.g., stroke; Every, Hochman, Becker, Kopecky, & Cannon, 2000).

Although based on current evidence or clinical guidelines, the clinical pathway details processes of care for the specific condition and, in noting any variances, highlights inefficiencies. Twenty-seven studies involving 11,398 participants were included in a meta-analysis of clinical pathway effectiveness (Rotter, Kinsman, James et al., 2010). Twenty studies compared stand-alone clinical pathways to usual care. These studies indicated a reduction in in-hospital complications and improved documentation. There was no evidence of differences in readmission to hospital or in-hospital mortality. Length of stay was the most commonly employed outcome measure with most studies reporting significant reductions. A decrease in hospital costs or charges was also observed. Seven studies compared clinical pathways as part of a multifaceted intervention with usual care. No evidence of differences were found between intervention and control groups. There are both strengths and limitations of the pathway process that an organization must consider in its development and use of the tool.

The development of a clinical pathway includes the following steps:

1. Select the topic. The topic should concentrate on high-volume, high-cost diagnoses and procedures; higher mortality; longer length of stay; or greater number of outcome variations. Surgical procedures are more suitable for pathways because of the predictable course of events that occur during the hospitalization.
2. Select a multidisciplinary team, including representatives from all groups that would be affected by the pathway. Without physician support of the pathway, it is unlikely to be successful and achieve any of the stated goals.
3. Evaluate and map the current process of care for the condition or procedure to identify current variation and create an idealized process.
4. Evaluate the current evidence in the literature. In the absence of best practices, comparison with other organizations, or benchmarking, is the best method to use.
5. Determine the clinical pathway form. This may be a hardcopy checklist placed in the patient's medical record or at bedside or an electronic tool capable of tracking variances.
6. Educate all users on how to use the tool and implement it. It is critical to define roles within the pathway for it to be successful.
7. Document and analyze variances that do not meet the expectation of the pathway. Identification of factors that contribute to variance and interventions to improve those factors are the key features of process improvement. Often, a case manager or other utilization

management staff member collects data on use of the pathway and variances. These data must then be analyzed and processes improved to achieve cost savings and QPI.

4. External Quality Awards

Viewing organizations as complex systems is consistent with the principles of quality pioneers such as Deming (2000) and Juran (1989) because QPI practices influence all processes, functions, and departments in an organization. Making changes in one process or department will entail changes in other processes, functions, and departments. Thus, effectiveness depends on alignment of the parts of the system.

Healthcare organizations are among the most complex entities, with ever-changing technology, new environmental pressures, and complicated relationships between professionals, disciplines, departments, and organizations. Therefore, research suggests that healthcare leaders must consider the science of complex adaptive systems to effectively manage and improve their organizations. *Complex* implies diversity, a wide variety of elements. *Adaptive* suggests the capacity to change, the ability to learn from experience. A *system* is a set of connected or interdependent things (Begun, Zimmerman, & Dooley, 2003).

One framework used to understand QPI in complex systems is the Baldrige National Health Care Criteria for Performance Excellence Framework, depicted in **Figure 22**. The Baldrige Award was created in 1987, named for former U.S. Secretary of Commerce Malcolm Baldrige in tribute to his managerial ability. The award is given to organizations demonstrating a commitment to quality excellence. This model displays the principles of QPI and shows the relationships between the structural, process, and outcome factors. Other common quality awards or designations are shown in **Table 11**.

There are other external awards that are not necessarily called quality awards but acknowledge high-performing organizations that demonstrate evidence of that performance according to defined criteria. Usually through a rigorous evaluation process, the organization is selected for the award, prize, or designation.

Figure 22. Baldrige National Health Care Criteria for Performance Excellence Framework 2011–2012

From "Baldrige Criteria for Performance Excellence Framework A Systems Perspective," in 2011–2012 Criteria for Performance Excellence (p. iv), 2011, Gaithersburg, MD: Baldrige Performance Excellence Program at the National Institute of Standards and Technology. Available at www.nist.gov/baldrige/publications/archive/upload/2008_Business_Nonprofit_Criteria.pdf. Adapted with permission.

Table 11. Common Quality Awards or Designations

Name	Owner	Eligible Organizations	Key Focus
Deming Prize	Union of Japanese Scientists and Engineers	Japan	Business total quality management performance Individuals, business units, organizations
Baldrige Performance Excellence Program	National Institute of Standards and Technology	National organizations (different sectors eligible, e.g., healthcare, education, business, government)	Performance excellence in 7 categories
Robert W. Carey Performance Excellence Award	Department of Veterans Affairs	Veterans Affairs organizations	Based on Baldrige criteria Performance excellence in 7 categories
State quality awards	States (public–private partnerships)	Individual states	Most similar to Baldrige criteria or criteria set by states
Magnet Recognition Program	American Nurses Credentialing Center	Healthcare organizations and systems	Nursing services and empirical outcomes for patients and nursing
Beacon Award for Excellence	American Association of Critical-Care Nurses	Critical care hospital units (high acuity and critically ill patients)	Hospital nursing units
Long-term care national quality awards	American Health Care Association (AHCA)/ National Center for Assisted Living (NCAL)	Long-term care and assisted living facilities	Commitment, achievement excellence
Shingo Prize for Operational Excellence	Utah State University	Any industry Any part of world	Customer focus and business results
John M. Eisenberg Patient Safety and Quality Awards	National Quality Forum and the Joint Commission	Organizations whose accomplishments are clearly linked to the principles Dr. Eisenberg promoted throughout his career	Healthcare quality and safety
Healthcare Quality Awards	National Association for Healthcare Quality	Individual professional recognition, state recognition	Healthcare quality and safety

Steps in evaluating readiness to apply for external quality awards include the following:

1. Demonstrate ownership and commitment to the cultural transformation for performance excellence.
2. Make the pursuit of quality an organizational commitment for the sake of improvement, not just to win an award.
3. Create the organization cultural transformation by upholding the standards in daily practice.
4. Identify the specific quality reward or recognition program and requirements.
5. Review the standards and criteria.
6. Determine eligibility.
7. Develop a team approach to self-assessment (facilitator or coordinator and subject matter experts).
8. Perform a self-assessment or gap analysis (**Table 12**) of current performance compared with the standards or criteria.

Table 12. Sample Framework for Performing a Gap Analysis

Standard	Importance	For High-Importance Areas			
	High, Medium, Low	Stretch (Strength) or Improvement Goal	What Action Is Planned?	By When?	Who Is Responsible?
Standard					
Strength or Evidence					
1.					
2.					
Opportunity for Improvement					
1.					
2.					
Standard					
Strength or Evidence					
1.					
2.					
Opportunity for Improvement					
1.					
2.					

From Healthcare Criteria for Performance Excellence: Optional self-analysis worksheet. NAHQ thanks the Baldrige Performance Excellence Program at the National Institute of Standards and Technology for use of text/graphics from the Criteria for Performance Excellence (Gaithersburg, MD: 2011). Available at www.nist.gov/baldrige/publications/hc_criteria.cfm

9. Identify strengths or evidence of compliance for each criterion.
10. Identify opportunities for improvement based on the criteria.
11. Prioritize findings from the self-assessment or gap analysis.
12. Plan a course of action to meet the standards.
13. Develop an action plan based on the priority for each criterion.
14. Perform ongoing feedback and update evidence of compliance.
15. Determine who will coordinate the application.
16. Complete an application.
17. Submit the application.
18. Plan for a site visit and documentation of evidence.
19. Sustain the process.
20. Integrate into daily operations.
21. Celebrate successes.

B. QPI Teams

An important structural element for QPI is creating a team-based organization. Because patient care involves multiple disciplines, the linchpin for improvement is an employee base that has regular communication and contact that allows them to coordinate and problem solve to continuously improve quality of care. The organization must develop an infrastructure within which the cycle of improvement can operate. One feature of this infrastructure is teams.

What is a team? A *team* is "a group of people who are interdependent with respect to information, resources, and skills and who seek to combine their efforts to achieve a common goal" (Thompson, 2000, p. 2).

1. Types of QPI Teams

There are many types of teams. **Figure 23** provides a mechanism for classifying teams along five major dimensions: purpose or mission, time, degree of autonomy, authority structure, and physical presence (Greenberg & Baron, 2003). In QPI, two teams are of great importance: steering committees (also called quality councils) and QPI teams. However, there are many other types of formal and informal teams.

Within QPI, there may be temporary project teams with a special focus on improvement, problem solving, or product development and often have both core and resource members. Core members participate throughout the project and often have complementary skills needed for the desired work output. Resource members may be critical only for specific phases of the project and may move in and out of the team. Other ongoing or functional work teams are usually permanent or may be long-standing. Natural work teams involve the people in a given work setting who share responsibility for a process, workflow, or type of work. A self-directed work team is a type of natural work team that shares many management responsibilities, such as scheduling work, managing budgets, evaluating performance, and hiring new team members. A process management team focuses on sharing responsibility for monitoring and controlling a work process, such as new product development. Members may rotate on and off the

Figure 23. Classification of Teams

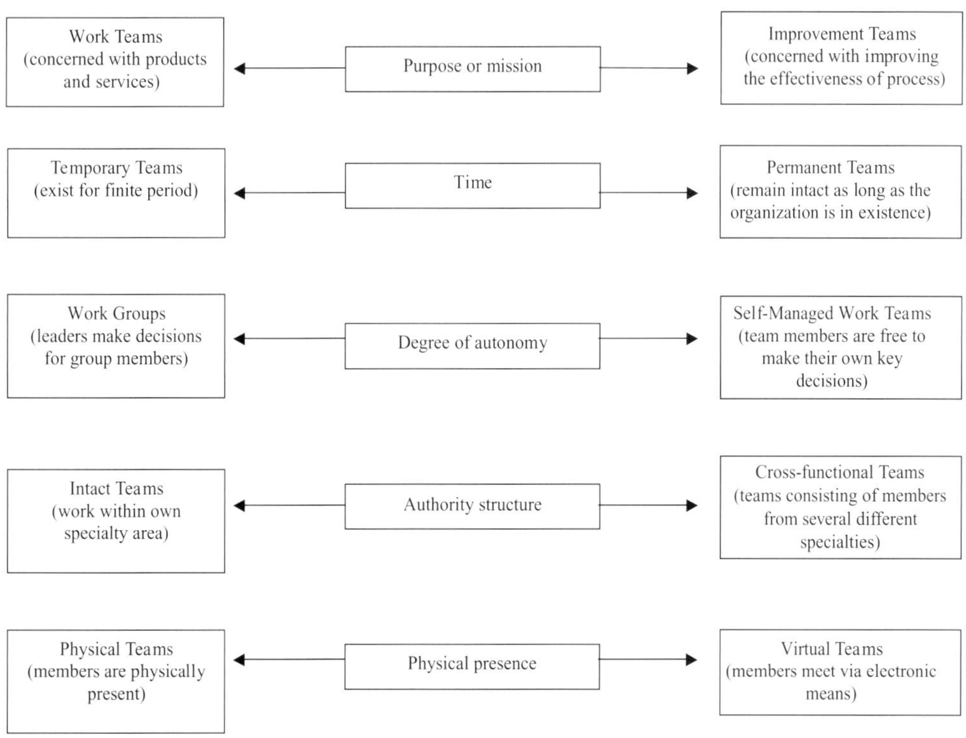

From Behavior in Organizations (8th ed.), by J. Greenberg & R. A. Baron, 2003, Upper Saddle River, NJ: Prentice Hall. Copyright 2003 by Prentice Hall. Reprinted with permission.

team based on their contributions (expertise). Virtual teams typically use technology-supported communications rather than face-to-face interactions to accomplish their tasks. They may cross boundaries, such as time zones, geography, and organizational units. Virtual teams can be either project teams or ongoing teams.

Steering Committees. Steering committees (often known as a quality councils) are permanent QPI teams consisting of cross-functional members. These committees are self-managed teams that provide direction and focus by identifying and prioritizing improvement opportunities in the organization. The role of the steering committee or quality council is to sustain, facilitate, and expand the QPI initiative based on the strategic plan. It should comprise top leaders in the organization, including medical staff. The main responsibilities of the quality council include

- lending legitimacy to the QPI efforts;
- maintaining organization focus on the identified goals and priorities;
- fostering teamwork for improvement;
- providing necessary resources (e.g., human, financial); and
- formulating QPI policies regarding quality and safety priorities, participation, annual self-assessments, and reward and recognition systems.

QPI Teams. QPI teams can be natural work teams, which are teams with members who work together each day in order to complete the task. These teams can be cross-functional, as with an operating room team, or intact, such as a team of nurses in a particular unit. Autonomy varies, but there typically is a leader. These teams can be temporary (e.g., brought together to solve a single problem) or permanent (e.g., continuous improvement teams).

2. When Should Teams Be Used?

Managers need to examine three aspects of the required task before deciding whether to use a team: task complexity, task interdependence, and task objectives (Luecke, 2004).

Tasks are considered to be complex when they involve large amounts of information, they are performed under conditions of high uncertainty, they contain many subtasks that require people with specialized skills and knowledge, and there are no standardized procedures for completing the tasks. Teams are important because they bring larger numbers of specialized individuals (i.e., subject matter experts) to carry the burden and offer greater diverse inputs that are more likely to result in more alternatives generated and more creative solutions. Creativity is particularly important when there are no standardized procedures and the environment is uncertain.

Task interdependence means that the work of one person is highly dependent on the work of others. Patient care typically involves a multitude of disciplines that must coordinate their work, and this requires intense communication. Teams therefore are appropriate, because this type of structure can foster communication between the various disciplines.

Finally, teams are appropriate to use when the task objectives are clear and time-bound. One approach for making task objectives clear is to develop a team charter. The charter should contain the following information (Schwarz, Landis, & Rowe, 1999):

- description of the process, why it needs improvement, and who is affected;
- development of criteria to demonstrate that the process has improved;
- timeline for meetings;
- resources available;
- structure of leadership (e.g., self-managed, leader-directed); and
- expected communication of progress, and results.

3. How Do Teams Develop or Grow?

Teams develop, mature, and change over time. Tuckman (1965) described four stages of development in one popular model with somewhat predictable stages. This classic framework continues to be used to this day.

Stage 1. Forming. During the first stage, the members try to get to know each other, agree on the goal or vision, and delegate tasks. They cautiously explore boundaries in an attempt to determine acceptable group behavior. Discussions focus on how to accomplish the tasks and the information and resources needed, and the team accomplishes little at this stage. This is a period of testing to find out what kind of behavior is appropriate. Members tend to defer to the leader or dominant member for guidance. In this stage, team leaders need to be directive and provide role clarification. Members get to know each other, agree on goals, and delegate tasks; members may feel anxiety, excitement, and uncertainty, and they may test boundaries of behavior. The team leader needs to be directive, with high-task relationships, and provide role clarification. The team depends on the leader during this learning stage. This stage is short if the tasks are clearly defined and easily achievable.

Stage 2. Storming. This second stage is where conflict typically arises. Members try to express their individuality and resist group pressures and influence. There often are emotional responses to group demands, especially if the group is under pressure to achieve results. To prevent the group from becoming stuck at this stage, leaders need to manage the conflict, not by suppressing it but by using it to energize the team. Conflict and tension often arise, and members assert their individual roles and compete for control. The leader moves to a coaching style of leadership. At this stage, reality sets in. There is the realization that the task may be difficult, they notice their lack of progress, and there is resistance to the task. Resources are applied to the task rather than education about the problem. People are willing to suggest tasks, and the leader then delegates the tasks. People do not take responsibility for problems, yet the team is building cohesion. This is probably the most difficult stage. Arguing, defensiveness, disunity, and tension are often evident.

Stage 3. Norming. In this stage, members develop close ties and a strong identity with the team. There is a shift from "I" to "we" and a willingness to accept the views of others. Team members develop feelings of mutual respect, harmony, and trust. Group standards and members' roles emerge. Leaders need to challenge the team members to continue to grow and guard against too much conformity to group norms. The team develops close ties and a strong identity; members develop harmony by avoiding conflict. Tentative constructive criticism is allowed.

A supporting leadership style evolves. Concern moves from silos to the interdisciplinary group. Members volunteer instead of just providing suggestions. There is an emerging leadership or ownership of functional roles by the members. There is acceptance of team rules, norms, and roles and finally optimism that things will work out. More harmony, cohesion, and discussion of team dynamics occur.

Stage 4. Performing. In the fourth stage, the team works harmoniously toward a common goal and is very productive. The team develops a functional but flexible structure, and roles are interrelated. Interpersonal conflicts are resolved, and the group is highly task oriented. In this stage, the leader needs to develop mechanisms for sharing leadership responsibilities. The team works harmoniously and gains insight into the team's process. Improvement of the team's process and team identification begins to predominate. The team is task oriented and accomplishes its work. Goal orientation is now optimized, and task competency is high. High morale, support, and appreciation come from team members. Roles diminish, and participation by all is encouraged. The team may begin to take on additional responsibilities and is functioning at an optimal level.

Not all teams progress through these four stages, and if they do, they probably move back and forth through the stages as new issues are identified. Nevertheless, the stages point to important developmental issues that have implications for team leaders, facilitators, and coaches. Lack of effectiveness often results from leadership and facilitation problems and a lack of clear goals and expectations. Teamwork components of cohesiveness, communication, role clarity, and goal clarity from *The Team Handbook* (Scholtes, Joiner, & Streibel, 2003) are integrated into these stages in **Table 13**.

4. Characteristics of Effective Teams

It is widely known that teams often fail to produce the results for which they were brought together. What makes a team successful? Abundant research and practice have demonstrated that the following are important predictors of team success (Campion, Medsker, & Higgs, 1993; George, 1995; Hackman, 1987; Katzenbach & Smith, 1994; Saunier & Hawk, 1994; Wageman, 1997):

- competent members with technical, problem-solving, interpersonal, and organizational skills;
- commitment to clear, common goals;
- standards of excellence;
- contributions from every member;
- collaborative environment (culture to support teamwork);
- leadership support;
- nonhierarchical structure; and
- external support and recognition.

Characteristics of effective and ineffective teams are further described in **Table 14**.

Four key traits can predict a team's success (Scholtes et al., 2003):

- cohesiveness,
- communication,
- clear roles, and
- clear goals.

Cohesiveness is the social glue that binds the team members together as a unit. Cohesiveness can be increased by the establishment of ground rules, or norms, addressing how meetings will be run, how team members will interact, and what kind of behavior is acceptable. Each member is expected to respect these rules, which usually prevents misunderstandings and disagreements. Balanced participation is encouraged to strengthen the team's cohesion. Because every team member has a stake in the achievements, everyone should participate in discussions and decisions, share commitment to the project's success, and contribute his or her talents. The use of brainstorming or a nominal group technique to obtain input from all team members during discussions is one method to encourage members to bond. When a team is cohesive, members are attracted to the team; find membership in the team to be a personally meaningful experience; enjoy the company of the other team members; support, nurture, and care for each other; feel free to share ideas and suggest ways to improve team function; feel they are using their unique skills for the benefit of the team; have a strong "we" feeling; and routinely develop creative solutions to problems.

Communication is the next key component to successful teams. Communication involves a full range of topics, including decision making and problem solving. Effective communication becomes easier once the team has developed a certain level of cohesiveness. Communication is key because further team development and effective functioning cannot occur without team communication. When a team is communicating effectively, team members always

- freely say what they feel and think;
- are always direct, truthful, respectful, and positive;
- openly discuss all decisions before they are made;
- handle conflict in a calm, caring, and healing manner;

Table 13. Team Roles

Sponsor	Sponsors are the formal leaders and prime movers of the project. They align resources and monitor progress. Sponsors hold others accountable to get on with change. The sponsor inspires the team members to say, "I believe in this project." Some project tasks require sponsors at multiple levels to obtain adequate resources and buy-in from the entire project team.
Champion	Champions are the respected opinion leaders who provide credibility to the project and are integral to the social structure. The champions are respected clinicians or staff with influence through clinical reputation or leadership qualities. Their experience provides credibility for the project team and task. They support the change and work for its implementation by speaking favorably about it and sharing their first-hand knowledge or experience.
Leader	Leaders guide the team to achieve successful outcomes and attain the established goals. They are responsible for guiding the team through the process to achieve the aim or goals. They provide direction and support. The team leader knows meeting procedures and has strong communication and interpersonal skills.
Timekeeper	Monitors meeting agendas, ensures the team is aware of the time allotted for each agenda item, and reminds the team when they go over the allotted time.
Process owner	The process owner is the leader among frontline staff directly involved in the process. This is the team member who is responsible and accountable for sustaining improvements during and after implementation. Ideally, the process owner should be someone with authority over frontline staff directly involved in the process evaluation.
Facilitator	Although facilitators (change agents or coaches) have no formal authority over other team members, they are instrumental in implementing the change through planning, helping, and facilitating. The facilitator is not vested in the project but is skilled in problem solving and adult learning and has good communication and interpersonal skills. As change agents, they are the technical experts on the team; they influence progress by gathering measurable data and information. They listen to the concerns of other team members and help remove barriers. They support the sponsors by advancing the team's work to goal achievement. They promote effective group dynamics and are concerned with how decisions are made. They may also serve as coaches or consultants. They keep the team on track. They provide expertise on using tools. Coaches focus on helping the team to learn rather than teaching them. The facilitator needs to have a clear perception of the facts and information and the ability to determine what is relevant. That ability includes an understanding of systems, dynamics, relationships between system components, and psychology. The facilitator, change agent, or coach needs to understand when and how emotions or desires distort one's perception.
Member	Actual representative on the team. Although project team composition varies, in most cases the project team includes the frontline staff (e.g., nurses, physicians, clerks, ancillary services staff) and area supervisors directly affected by the project task. To identify these personnel, consider all relevant stakeholders to the process. The ideal team size is 8–12 people. Unless necessary, team size should not exceed 15 people. They are able to collect data and information related to the process of focus. For the stakeholders not represented, develop a communication mechanism (team minutes, session report) and designate one or more people to disseminate this information regularly. Chosen team members must be able to commit to attend team meetings and meet their responsibilities.
Scribe	This role may be assigned to one person or rotated between members. The role includes documenting minutes of meetings and other recordkeeping activities.

Table 14. Team Characteristics

Effective Teams	Ineffective Teams
Mutual agreement and identification with respect to the team goal	Does not distinguish between facts, opinions, and feelings
Open communication between members	Does not separate idea generation from idea evaluation
Mutual trust and support	Prematurely closes discussion before all alternatives are identified
Management of human differences	Dominated by aggressive members
Selective use of the team	Fails to assign specific responsibilities
Appropriate member skills	Does not review minutes, tasks, or due dates
Leadership	Works on problems that are outside the scope of the team
Values and goals of the members interpreted as needs and values of the team	Exhibits uncertainty about the team's direction
Team believes it can accomplish the impossible	Launches many improvement projects without clear objectives
Understands the value of constructive team cohesiveness and how to use it	Fails to apply discussion skills
Mutual influence between members and the leader	Hides a secret agenda
Exhibits clear goals, purposes, discussions, and decisions	Relies on one person to manage discussion without sharing responsibility
Agrees on the goal	Discusses the project outside the meeting rather than bringing issues to the team
Has formally defined roles	Repeats points of discussion
Revises plan as needed	Concedes to opinions rather than fact-based data
Uses tool to map the process and project steps	Uses majority rule rather than consensus in disagreements
Effectively uses talents of members	Uses decision by default, with silence assumed as consent
Balances participation of all members	Avoids certain topics
Discusses issues openly	Does not acknowledge ground rules
Clarifies ideas or issues	Has recurring differences on acceptable behavior
Uses consensus-based decision making	Has conflicting expectations
Uses data for problem solving	Does not attend to clues or shifts in the team mood
Applies resources and training throughout the project	Makes remarks that discount someone's behavior or contribution

- openly explore options to solve problems when they arise;
- do not gossip about each other; and
- do not have a hidden agenda.

Good, clear communication depends on how well information is passed between team members. Ideally, team members should speak clearly, directly, and succinctly. They should ask questions in an inviting way. Members should listen actively and avoid interrupting when others are speaking. Teams should encourage all members to use the skills and practices that make discussions and meetings more effective. Team members should initiate discussions, seek information and opinions, suggest procedures, elaborate on ideas, complete assignments on time, and summarize. Team leaders and facilitators act as gatekeepers during communication by managing member participation, keeping discussion focused, and resolving differences creatively. Considering the stage of team development, such as storming, leaders and facilitators may need to ease tension and work through difficulties. Communication also includes well-defined decision-making procedures. A team should always be aware of the different ways it reaches decisions. The team should discuss how decisions will be made, explore important issues by polling, test for agreement, and use data as the basis for decisions. Occasionally, the team may want to designate a member to observe team interactions and give feedback on how decisions are made so the group can talk about any changes it needs to make. Team members should also be sensitive to nonverbal communication. This includes seeing, hearing, and feeling the team dynamics.

Role clarity is the next area to facilitate team success. The role of team member supersedes individual professional roles. Although professional roles brought to the team give the team its potential strength, it is also important for team development that individuals feel equally valued. In addition, team members should know who is doing what and what other team members expect of them. When a team achieves role clarity, members feel that accomplishments of the team are placed above those of individuals, understand the roles and responsibilities of all other team members, and have a clear understanding of what other team members expect of them. Teams should also have an identified facilitator. Facilitation requires skills that are both art and science. A skilled facilitator guides group process in an unbiased manner ensuring that the meeting agenda is carried out and decisions are responsibly reached with independent contributions from all team members.

The final component of team development to become a fully functioning and high-performing team is clearly defining team goals and the means used to reach these goals. When a team achieves goal clarity, team members agree on what the real work of the team is, clearly understand the goals, agree on how to reach the goals, and agree on clear criteria for evaluating the outcomes of the team. Teams operate most efficiently when they tap everyone's talents and when all members understand their duties and know who is responsible for what issues and tasks. Goal clarity begins with a charter.

Successful teams are one of the most important aspects of effective organizational functioning and QPI. Two special team types have patient safety as their main focus but include essential elements of teams that increase their ability to address patient safety and error reduction. The first is Team Strategies and Tools to Enhance Performance and Patient Safety (TeamSTEPPS®; **Figure 24**), a teamwork system designed for healthcare professionals. This is an evidence-based teamwork system designed to improve communication and teamwork skills. Team members learn four primary teamwork skills: leadership, communication, situation monitoring, and mutual support. Three types of team outcomes are desired: performance, knowledge, and attitudes.

The TeamSTEPPS model is based on lessons learned, change models, the literature of quality and patient safety, and culture change. Phase 1 assesses an organization's readiness for undertaking the initiative. Phase 2 includes planning, training, and implementation; options in this phase include tools and strategies. Phase 3 sustains and spreads improvements in teamwork performance, clinical processes, and outcomes (AHRQ, n.d.).

The second special type of team is Crew Resource Management (CRM). A specific CRM training program based on airline safety was developed for healthcare. Although the team is focused on patient safety, the effectiveness of team functioning is a first critical component (American Combatives, 2009). Additional elements include a focus on the patient safety mindset and high-reliability functioning. The team learns skills in decision making under stressful situations through continued practice, simulation, and use of checklists to embed teamwork behaviors into daily work and provide numerous opportunities to practice the desired behaviors.

For those organizations employing Six Sigma or lean QPI methods, a *Workout* is a fast track change acceleration process developed originally at General Electric. The Workout is conducted by a group of team members in a short period of time (hours or days; Zuzelo, 2010).

Figure 24. The TeamSTEPPS® Model

From "TeamSTEPPS®: National Implementation," by the Agency for Healthcare Research and Quality, U.S. Department of Health & Human Services, 2012, Rockville, MD: AHRQ. Available at http://teamstepps.ahrq.gov/teamstepps logo.htm.

C. Evaluating Team Performance

Because teams are so important to organizational operations, how should teams be evaluated? Three key actions determine the success of any team:

- developing shared goals and methods to accomplish outcomes,
- developing methods and skills to communicate and make decisions across systems and organizations, and
- engaging leadership that balances getting input and making decisions, so work moves ahead.

Team performance also requires formal evaluation. In general, evaluation of a team includes three criteria:

- Productivity or results: The extent to which the goals were met. Did the team accomplish what it set out to do and within the defined time frame?
- Satisfaction of team members: It is important that team members be able to work together in the future. To the extent that members are satisfied with the team, they will be more likely to work well together in the future.
- Individual growth: The extent to which individual members developed professionally by serving as team members.

A more formalized manner of evaluating team performance includes the following process criteria:

- Organizational alignment:
  - Does the team have statements of mission, vision, values, structures, roles, and goals?
  - Does the team have a charter? Is the goal important to the organization's strategic priorities?
- Goal clarity: Are there clearly stated goals, and do actions exist to achieve the goals?
- Leadership: Is there clear leadership support of the team?

- Roles: Have team roles been defined?
- Norms: Does the team have defined ground rules and abide by them?
- Team participation: Do all members of the team participate and share tasks?
- Team meetings: Are team meetings organized with agendas, time frames, action plans, and decisions?
- Competency to perform tasks: Are members trained to work on tasks?
- Communication: Is communication open, honest, and constructive?
- Atmosphere: Is the atmosphere warm, accepting, and supportive for all team members?
- Decision making: Does the team achieve consensus on decisions and look at multiple alternatives before reaching a decision?
- Problem solving: Is the team able to validate problem identification before moving to a solution by using sound data and tools?
- Conflicts: Does the team have a process for constructively managing conflict?
- Performance management: Does the team manage its performance, or must management intervene?
- Work tools and training: Has the team been trained on tools and data management to function effectively?
- Boundary management: Has the team developed relationships with other teams, stakeholders, and customers?

D. Coordinating and Participating in QPI Projects

Healthcare quality professionals play an important role in leading or facilitating QPI projects. Many different types of improvement projects may be chartered. They vary in breadth, scope, and duration. There are also different names that may be assigned to projects, but they all can be categorized under the umbrella of QPI. For example, there may be rapid process improvement teams, green belt project teams, black belt project teams, lean projects, Six Sigma projects, and redesign projects. All are similar in their basic approach. The types of tools and level of statistical analysis may also vary by type of team. Depending on the complexity of the project, a simple action plan may be sufficient, or the use of a Gantt or PERT chart for project management may be needed.

A basic approach and actual steps in a QPI project include the following:

1. Alignment with priorities and strategic goals and objectives.
   - This first step ensures the leaders support this project because it aligns with the strategic goals and performance improvement priorities and are willing to devote resources to it.
   - A team charter is usually written at this point and describes the scope, boundaries, expected results, and resources used by a process improvement team. The individual or group who formed the team usually provides the charter. Sometimes the process owner or the team members develop a charter. A charter is always needed for a team working on a process that crosses departmental lines. A charter may not be necessary for a team that is improving a process found solely within a work center or office space.
   - Basic team functions are identified, including
     - members of the team,
     - roles within the team,
     - meeting schedule,
     - project timeline,

  - resources available and needed to complete the improvement project, and
  - expected communication of progress and results.
- A clear defined aim must be identified for the team to work toward a common goal.
- Analysis of baseline performance and problem identification is needed to determine the level of improvement.
- A map of the process (current and ideal) should be developed.

2. Description of the process: why it needs improvement and who is affected.
3. Development of criteria to demonstrate that the process is improved.
4. Measurement of success; this includes the numerator and denominator for a percentage, rate, or other weighted measure.
5. Changes to be tested and implemented.
6. Tests of change supported by data collection, analysis, and reporting.
7. Control or methods to sustain the change.
8. Results or outcomes of the project.
9. Reporting of the project and results to leaders, the organization, or others.
10. Evaluation tools for the team process.

E. Organizational Reviews and Audits

Performance monitoring is an important role of QPI staff. A number of areas have been identified in accreditation standards, regulatory requirements, and organizational demands. Generally, these areas have been identified as high risk to patient safety and quality of care. The areas that are most common will be presented. General criteria to be considered for a review or audit include the following:

- Was the intervention used?
- Was it performed properly according to specific criteria?
- Was it performed safely?
- Was there any adverse effect or outcome to the patient?
- Was staff competent to perform the intervention?
- Was it effective (this may include cost effectiveness)?
- Was there a better alternative to the intervention?

These general criteria will be applied to several areas to demonstrate what should be considered for monitoring or auditing the specific process.

Medication Use. Safe medication practices, including medication use evaluation, pharmacy and therapeutics, adverse drug reactions, and adverse drug events, are reviewed in healthcare organizations. The types of medications and the setting in which they are used will indicate which medications are high risk, high alert, frequently used, and most vulnerable to underuse, overuse, and misuse. Thousands of drugs are currently on the market. Many are hazardous to use but have beneficial effects for patients. Organizations should identify the drugs they provide in a standard formulary and identify methods to obtain nonformulary items. The use of nonformulary medications should be monitored, usually by the pharmacy, to determine cost-effective, safe medications for administration and ways to integrate new medications into use.

High-risk medications include antibiotics, opioids, insulin, anticoagulants, and chemotherapy. High-risk populations may include infants and children, frail older adults, immunocompromised patients, critically ill patients, and transplant recipients.

The purpose of medication use monitoring is to improve the efficiency and effectiveness of medication use and the appropriate use of medication. Because of the frequent use of medications in healthcare, ongoing monitoring is needed. Priorities for monitoring are based on the numbers of patients affected (volume), the degree of risk associated with the drug's use (risk), the degree to which the medication is known to be problem prone, and other criteria developed by the medical staff. The usual steps in measuring improvement include

1. prescribing appropriate medication,
2. preparing and dispensing medications,
3. administering medications, and
4. monitoring the effects of mediations on patients.

Trends and patterns of usage can be presented in several different ways, which may include a description of use in the four steps just listed. Trends can be described in terms of specific medication types, such as antibiotic usage, and compared with antibiograms for specific organisms. Patterns also can be presented relative to overuse, underuse, and misuse. **Table 15** uses the basic monitoring criteria to illustrate medication monitoring of a specific case that can be used to aggregate the data into trends.

Blood Use. The administration of blood and blood products is a high-risk aspect of care. Staff must consider the risk and the therapeutic benefit, including the risk of bloodborne pathogens, transfusion reactions, and transfusion errors. It is also a high-cost item. The key elements to be monitored include ordering, distribution (availability and timeliness of administration), handling and dispensing, administration, and monitoring of the effects on patients. Individual cases are reviewed (**Table 16**), and then an evaluation of blood usage practices for providers and the organization can be performed. An evaluation might include blood that is administered when not indicated, not administered when indicated, or administered incorrectly. Specific standards from the College of American Pathologists and the American Association of Blood Banks may be useful for evaluating transfusion services.

Restraints. Restraint use is another high-risk procedure that may be used in certain populations. It is no longer allowed in the long-term care setting but may be used in acute hospitals for medical-surgical populations, for inpatient behavioral health populations, and in the emergency department for highly unpredictable patients and situations. Some national and state organizations are calling for the eradication of restraint use in behavioral health settings altogether because of high-profile adverse events related to their use. Recently developed core measures in inpatient behavioral health include metrics for restraint and seclusion use.

The CMS has established specific rules related to restraint usage, and these have been adopted by the Joint Commission, which has deemed status with CMS. The monitoring of this process includes each episode of restraint application (**Table 17**). Often a checklist is used to ensure that all required components are met. If a checklist or template is used, each episode can be monitored easily according to criteria. An aggregate summary allows the organization to determine any trends in usage. Such trends may reveal patterns associated with

- time of day or day of week in which restraint usage may be higher, such as nights or weekends;
- units in which restraint usage may be higher, such as geropsychiatric units or units with higher numbers of patients with tubes and other devices; and
- providers whose ordering practices reveal higher restraint use.

Operative and Invasive Procedure Review. Operative, invasive, and noninvasive procedures are important diagnostic and therapeutic interventions. They often pose risk to patients and must be monitored systematically (**Table 18**). Aspects to be considered for monitoring include the following:

Table 15. Medication Monitoring

General Criteria	Specific Criteria
Was the intervention used?	What class or type of medication is being monitored (e.g., antibiotic, opioid, insulin, anticoagulant)?
Was it performed properly according to specific criteria?	Was the medication administered in accordance with policy, criteria, or current evidence (e.g., was the proper antibiotic preoperatively administered and within 1 hour)?
Was it performed safely?	Was the medication administered safely (e.g., should the medication be administered by an infusion device to control rate, should it be administered in a central versus peripheral site, was it diluted properly)?
Was there any adverse effect or outcome to the patient?	Were there any adverse effects to patients (e.g., medication reactions or complications, allergies, errors, interactions with other medications or foods)?
Was staff competent to perform the intervention?	Was the staff who administered the medication competent in the procedure (e.g., does the route of administration require special knowledge and skill, does the type of medication require a certain setting for observation, is there a specific competency)?
Was it effective?	Did the medication achieve the desired result or an untoward result?
Was there a better alternative to the intervention?	Were there clearly documented indications for use of the medication? If the medication is high risk, high alert, or nonformulary, was there documentation on usage?

Table 16. Blood Usage Monitoring

General Criteria	Specific Criteria
Was the intervention used?	Was blood or blood components administered?
Was it performed properly according to specific criteria?	Was the order for the blood products clear and documented in the medical record? Was blood administration performed according to defined policy including vital signs before, during, and after administration? Were proper tubing, filters, and administration devices used?
Was it performed safely?	Was the patient monitored during the administration? Was the rate of administration in accordance with policy, orders, and the patient's condition?
Was there any adverse effect or outcome to the patient?	Were there any adverse reactions to the administration (immediate or delayed)? If there was a reaction, was the response in accordance with policy?
Was staff competent to perform the intervention?	Were the staff who administered the blood products competent in the procedure (is there a specific competency)?
Was it effective?	Was the most appropriate blood product administered for the patient's condition?
Was there a better alternative to the intervention?	Was there a review of lab results, vital signs, and other results before the order to determine whether the particular blood product was indicated (e.g., iron, watchful waiting)? Was there a review of any special considerations before administration, such as religious beliefs?

Table 17. Restraint Use Monitoring

General Criteria	Specific Criteria
Was the intervention used?	Were restraints applied to the patient (what type of restraint and what limb or body part was restrained)? Was the restraint considered medical–surgical or behavioral health?
Was it performed properly according to specific criteria?	Were restraints applied properly in accordance with policy, CMS regulations, and Joint Commission standards? Was there compliance with requirements for orders, timeliness, trial releases, alternatives, initial face-to-face assessment, and ongoing monitoring?
Was it performed safely?	Were restraints applied safely so that the patient was not at risk for injury or harm?
Was there any adverse effect or outcome to the patient?	Were there any adverse effects (e.g., physical, emotional) to the patient related to the application of restraints?
Was staff competent to perform the intervention?	Were the staff who applied the restraints competent in the procedure (is there a specific competency)?
Was it effective?	Did the use of the restraints achieve the desired result?
Was there a better alternative to the intervention?	Were other alternatives tried before restraints applied (and documented)? Was seclusion used with restraints?

Table 18. Operative and Invasive Procedure Monitoring

General Criteria	Specific Criteria
Was the intervention used?	What was the surgical or invasive procedure performed?
Was it performed properly according to specific criteria?	Were there documented indications for the procedure? Was the patient properly informed of risks, benefits, and alternatives?
Was it performed safely?	Was the procedure performed according to policy, guidelines, or other criteria?
Was there any adverse effect or outcome to the patient?	Was there any adverse effect on the patient before, during, or after the procedure? Was any action taken to prevent, mitigate, or respond to an adverse event (e.g., preprocedure positioning to prevent injury, postprocedure X ray if a retained object was suspected)?
Was staff competent to perform the intervention?	Were staff performing the procedure competent? Were providers privileged to perform the procedure?
Was it effective?	What was the final result for the patient?
Was there a better alternative to the intervention?	Was the procedure elective, urgent, or emergent? Were all possible options considered and discussed with the patient? Were specialists consulted if needed? Was the procedure performed in the right setting (e.g., inpatient or outpatient, or in a specialty hospital, or a hospital that performs a high volume of procedures vs. a hospital that infrequently performs a procedure, especially one of high risk and complexity)?

- selection of the appropriate procedures,
- patient preparation for procedures,
- performance of the procedure and patient monitoring,
- postprocedure care,
- preprocedure and postprocedure patient education,
- preprocedure and postprocedure diagnostic discrepancies,
- moderate sedation monitoring, and
- complications or adverse events related to the procedure.

Procedures always carry the risk of complications even when performed properly. Risk is greater with procedures performed when not indicated, not performed when indicated, and performed poorly or incorrectly. Outcomes are influenced by clinical performance of all preprocedure processes; clinical performance of the procedure; and patient monitoring before, during, and after the procedure.

Other factors may also be monitored as indicators of possible quality-of-care problems (Griffin & Resar, 2009):

- return to surgery;
- change in procedure;
- admission to ICU postoperatively (unplanned);
- intubation, reintubation, or use of bilevel positive airway pressure in postanesthesia care unit;
- X ray intraoperatively or in postanesthesia care unit;
- intraoperative or postoperative death;
- mechanical ventilation more than 24 hours after surgery;
- intraoperative administration of epinephrine, norepinephrine, naloxone, or flumazepil;
- postoperative increase in troponin levels greater than 1.5 ng/ml;
- injury repair or removal of organ during operative procedure (unplanned); and
- occurrence of any operative complication.

Several national databases allow comparisons of organizational data with risk-adjusted surgical cases for observed-to-expected ratios of morbidity and mortality. This allows the organization to use an external comparison or benchmark to assess its rate of complications as a trigger or threshold for action (e.g., National Surgical Quality Improvement Program; Chevron Supplier Quality Improvement Process, Society of Thoracic Surgeons National Database).

Cardiopulmonary Resuscitation (CPR) Monitoring. CPR monitoring and the outcomes are important to include in any QPI program (**Table 19**). Cardiopulmonary resuscitation is defined as the application of chest compressions, defibrillation, and artificial respirations or rescue breathing. One consideration in CPR monitoring is whether the patient exhibited any signs or symptoms that should have been identified for early intervention before a full arrest occurred. In the event that CPR must be performed, there are specific guidelines on chest compressions, airway maintenance and breathing, defibrillation, and medications. Advanced care and treatment depend on the setting and patient's underlying condition. A national registry for data on CPR events collects detailed information on exact interventions, times, and results (including electrocardiograms). The use of a registry allows comparison of data on process and outcome measures.

Table 19. Cardiopulmonary Resuscitation (CPR) Monitoring

General Criteria	Specific Criteria
Was the intervention used?	Was CPR performed?
Was it performed properly according to specific criteria?	Was CPR performed correctly and promptly in accordance with basic life support or advanced cardiac life support guidelines?
Was it performed safely?	Was CPR performed safely (e.g., consider the location of the victim, defibrillation, and other safety factors)?
Was there any adverse effect or outcome to the patient?	What was the outcome (immediate, defined intervals, at discharge)?
Was staff competent to perform the intervention?	Were staff trained and certified in the proper level of response? Was certification current?
Was it effective?	Were compressions and rescue breathing effective in sustaining perfusion?
Was there a better alternative to the intervention?	Were there early warning signs for rapid response team to intervene before full arrest?

Mortality and Morbidity Review. Review of mortality and morbidity is often based on specific criteria. For mortality, a review of expected or unexpected mortality (observed vs. expected) is performed by condition, within specific time frames (e.g., immediately in the operating room, in the hospital setting, or within 30 days after discharge), and based on inclusion and exclusion criteria. For example, patients who are expected to die based on a terminal condition with a Do Not Resuscitate order, who are in hospice, or who have an end-stage condition are usually excluded from review. Other mortalities are then reviewed as outcomes that can provide information about the quality of care provided. Similarly, complications are also reviewed, and the criteria for cases and conditions to be reviewed are established by the medical staff. Individual cases are then identified and reviewed, and aggregated reports are trended to identify opportunities for improvement. Comparisons of trends can be made internally over time or externally compared with national databases.

Morbidity and mortality data are often risk adjusted to compare similar patients (usually with similar conditions, procedures, or DRGs). National databases allow comparison of morbidity and mortality using a risk-adjusted model (e.g., all Patient Refined DRGs). Typical occurrence screening examples for mortality include

- death within 24 hours of admission to a hospital;
- death within 72 hours of transfer out of special care unit;
- lack of documentation of deterioration during 48 hours preceding death;
- failure of physician to respond to notification of change in patient's condition during 48 hours preceding death;
- lack of documentation indicating death was expected;
- lack of concordance between premortem and postmortem diagnosis;
- clinically significant incident or occurrence within 72 hours of death;
- clinically significant complication of surgical procedure within 72 hours of death;
- clinically significant complication of invasive procedure within 72 hours of death;
- death during surgery;
- unplanned organ removal during operative procedure within 2 months preceding death;

- surgical procedure to repair a perforation, laceration, or other injury of an organ during an invasive procedure within 2 months preceding death;
- repeat of any surgical procedure within 2 months preceding death;
- myocardial infarction within 24 hours of a surgical or invasive procedure;
- death within 48 hours of elective surgical procedure; and
- lack of concordance between preoperative and postoperative diagnosis.

F. Infection Prevention and Control Processes

The goal of the infection prevention and control (IPC) program is to identify and reduce the risks of acquiring and transmitting endemic and epidemic infections among patients, employees, physicians, other IPCs, contractors, volunteers, students, and visitors. This includes both direct patient care and support staff. The three major aspects of the IPC program are surveillance, prevention, and control.

The usual responsibilities of the IPC program include

- definitions of healthcare-associated infections (HAIs),
- definitions of data elements,
- rationale for surveillance method selected,
- description of patient population studied,
- data collection methods,
- quality control procedures for data validation,
- responsibility,
- systems for reporting and follow-up,
- reporting to public health authorities, and
- documentation of employee infections of epidemiologic significance.

The prevention and control methods used in IPC include

- policies and procedures to protect and prevent infections;
- defined barrier precautions;
- orientation and ongoing education of staff;
- reporting to public health officials;
- methods for screening and documentation of epidemiologically significant infections;
- systems for required waste identification;
- use of personal protective equipment and supplies:
  - patient care supplies and equipment (e.g., sterile and nonsterile supplies, hand hygiene facilities),
  - protective apparel, and
  - engineering controls;
- precautions used to reduce the risk of infection:
  - surveillance, and
  - assessment and analysis of infection rates;
- decontamination, high-level disinfection, and sterilization:
  - reusable medical equipment,
  - policies and procedures, and
  - processes identified:

» principles of asepsis;
» disinfection, sterilization;
» sanitation of rooms, equipment;
» selection, use, and cleaning of personal protective equipment; and
» traffic control.

The IPC program is based on a risk assessment of the organization. This assessment includes factors such as

- geographic location of the organization,
- populations within the region or organization and level of risk (e.g., neonates, infants and children, and patients in various ICUs),
- volume of patients served and volume of conditions (e.g., number of patients with positive human immunodeficiency virus, tuberculosis, and colonized with methicillin-resistant *Staphylococcus aureus* [MRSA]),
- clinical focus of programs (e.g., types of surgeries and invasive procedures, immunocompromised patients such as patients on chemotherapy, transplant patients),
- number of employees (often encompasses employee health services), and
- scope of services provided (e.g., acute, ambulatory, long-term, and home care).

After the risk assessment is completed, priorities are identified and strategies to prevent or mitigate problems are determined. In many healthcare settings the prevention of HAIs in high-risk units (ICU, neonatal and pediatric ICU, transplant units, dialysis units, and surgical units) is a key responsibility. These HAIs must be monitored and analyzed to determine trends and ways to reduce their occurrence. The types of surveillance for IPC programs include total house, priority directed, targeted, problem oriented, and outbreak response.

The most important factor in monitoring prevention of HAIs is proper hand hygiene. The monitoring of hand hygiene using either Centers for Disease Control or World Health Organization criteria is a requirement of the Joint Commission and one of the National Patient Safety Goals.

Specific monitoring is performed for surgical-site infections and for device-related infections including ventilator-associated pneumonia, central line–associated bloodstream infection, and catheter-associated urinary tract infection.

Another key role is to identify communicable diseases, control outbreaks when identified in patients, and report specific results to the public health department. One preventive measure for controlling certain outbreaks is immunization programs conducted in collaboration with occupational health staff. These might include vaccination for hepatitis B, influenza, pneumonia, and other viral diseases. The infection preventionist is also responsible for monitoring epidemiologically important and multidrug-resistant organisms such as MRSA, *Clostridium difficile*, and vancomycin-resistant *Enterococcus*.

G. Departmental Reviews

The organization should have an organization-wide plan for performance improvement. Examples of key activities and quality control methods should be defined for each service. There are numerous regulations at the federal, state, and local level that govern quality control monitoring and reporting. This is especially true for diagnostic services such as pathology and laboratory services, radiology, nuclear medicine, and pharmacy. Content experts in these services should lead the identification of regulations or other requirements and the specific quality control processes and measures that must be maintained. The requirements may include provisions for employee exposure monitoring, including issuance of individual radiology badges or devices. Quality management personnel are often involved in the direct monitoring within services or the aggregation of data or reports from these services. The unit or service level is considered a microsystem, and it is at this level that change happens and improvements generally occur.

A format that can be used for a service-level QPI plan includes the following tasks:

- identifying customers served;
- describing services provided;
- developing performance improvement priorities at the service level, aligned with the organization's goals and strategic plan;
- identifying any requirements related to performance improvement, quality control, and quality monitoring (e.g., accreditation standards, regulations, device monitoring, quality control);
- selecting valid and reliable metrics for the service;
- developing a monitoring plan (e.g., sample, frequency, reporting);
- analyzing the results;
- evaluating the performance; and
- improving the performance.

A standard format can make the development of service plans or quality monitoring across multiple services and sites more efficient and effective for tracking, trending, and reporting.

H. Health Records

Healthcare facilities and clinical staff who treat patients are required to maintain adequate medical records to serve as a basis for planning care and for communicating about patients' conditions and treatments with other healthcare providers. The medical or health record serves other purposes as well. For example, medical records are reviewed by administrative staff performing quality, utilization, and risk management (RM) functions and by physicians engaged in peer review. Outside organizations also use the medical record for matters relating to payment and accreditation. In malpractice cases, the medical record serves as the major source of evidence about the care the patient received. Information contained in medical records also is used in retrospective clinical research. If protected health information (PHI) is collected for research, institutional review board approval is needed.

Healthcare organizations should have a clear policy about who may have access to medical records, whether those records are written, computerized, or otherwise maintained. Policy statements also should make clear what, other than actual medical records, constitutes a portion of the record. For example, with the advent of and frequent use of videotaping of procedures or fetal heart monitoring strips, it is important to address (based on state law and legal advice) whether such media are part of the medical record.

The legal basis for confidentiality derives from the physician-patient privilege, set forth by statute in almost all states. This is one of several relationships recognized as special by law. The preservation of confidentiality is viewed as essential to the maintenance of the relationship. The need for confidentiality in the physician-patient relationship gives rise to a legal privilege. This means that, absent a patient authorization or waiver or an overriding law or public policy, medical information about a patient is protected from the process known as *discovery*, through which parties to a lawsuit normally can compel disclosure of relevant evidence. In certain states, the physician-patient privilege is extended beyond physicians to protect the patient's relationship with other healthcare practitioners (e.g., psychologists, clinical social workers, clinical nurse specialists, nurse practitioners).

1. Information Covered by Privilege

This information extends beyond oral communication between practitioner and patient to cover written entries in the patient's medical record, as well as X rays, cardiograph or fetal monitoring strips, laboratory results, and other information about a patient's condition that is kept by the individual provider or healthcare institution. Information that is privileged must satisfy the following conditions:

- It must have been communicated in the context of the physician-patient relationship.
- It must have been given with the expectation that it remain confidential.
- It must be necessary for the diagnosis and treatment of the patient.

In understanding the function of the medical record to provide information about the patient's care, treatment, and services and to serve as the method of sharing this information between caregivers, there are monitoring processes to ensure the integrity, accuracy, and completeness of the record and reflect the pertinent clinical documentation. The medical record may be a hard copy document or electronic (or a combination). With current legislation demanding that healthcare organizations implement electronic health records, there has been an increase in electronic records.

The monitoring of the medical record usually includes elements in several categories:

- Required documentation content: The requirements vary by setting, procedure, and even profession. For example, the requirements for a treatment plan will be different for an acute care hospital and a long-term-care facility. The requirements for surgery with general anesthesia will be different from those for an outpatient procedure with moderate sedation. Each facility must first identify the required content for the record and then develop a process to monitor important elements. Checklists, databases, or other tools make this process more efficient. This step often reflects the presence or absence of the required content.
- Timeliness of documentation: The next requirement is the time requirement of specific documentation. Most common elements monitored for timeliness include history and physical, preoperative and postoperative notes, and discharge summaries. This step reflects whether the documentation met or did not meet the required timeline.
- Appropriateness of documentation (clinical pertinence): The monitoring of clinical pertinence requires an assessment of the documentation in terms of the patient's condition, diagnostic results, intervention procedures, vital signs, and other information. This review may determine that documentation was appropriate or not appropriate to the standard of care, key elements of the assessment, treatment plan, interventions, and medication management.

I. Medical Peer Review

The data contained in a medical record are private and highly confidential. Policies and procedures clearly define who may have access to a medical record and under what circumstances, in accordance with medical staff bylaws, hospital policy, and applicable laws and regulations. Because of the complexity of those issues, consultation from general counsel regarding national and state statutes is critical. Practitioner profiles can be maintained as a part of the credentials file or in a separate locked file. Most states have laws governing medical peer review and its activities. When applicable, files, their contents, and meeting minutes should be marked as "Confidential: Peer Review According to Statute X" or with a simple "Confidential" stamp.

A mechanism also should be developed to track activity on each individual practitioner profile. A log or sign-out sheet attached to each file should contain the date of request, reason for request or review, name of person reviewing, and any pertinent notes such as requests for copies of the contents. Policies and procedures define the circumstances under which copies of contents are made, such as individual physician requests. In accordance with medical staff bylaws and rules and regulations, a mechanism for release of information with specification of contents to be disclosed should be developed. This mechanism is in response to evaluation of a practitioner's competence for appointment and reappointment to other healthcare institutions.

Minutes of QPI activities usually are protected under the medical peer review statutes. Therefore, maintenance of confidentiality of records extends beyond credentialing to the entire QPI program in the organization.

Peer review is the review of an episode of care conducted for the purpose of improving the quality of patient care or the use of healthcare resources. It is a process protected by statute in most states, although this varies, and by federal statute for federal healthcare facilities. A peer is generally defined as a healthcare professional who has comparable education, training, experience, licensure, or similar clinical privileges or scope of practice. The peer review process includes a case review according to criteria established by the medical staff. These reviews may include an assessment of the degree to which a standard was met or if providers in the same situation would have acted in the same manner. These ratings may be noted as a score or level number for tracking purposes or as a trigger for FPPE when continued quality concerns are identified. Results may be trended by individual provider performance or by organization system. Usually, a peer review committee manages the review and reporting function as a subcommittee of the medical executive committee. Participation in peer review is one way medical staff members are involved in measuring, assessing, and improving performance of licensed practitioners.

Medical staff identify criteria or circumstances that initiate a peer review, set time frames for the review to occur, identify reviewers, and provide mechanisms for participation by the person whose performance is being reviewed. Both outcomes and processes should be measured.

An effective peer review process will include the following elements:

- Consistency: Peer review is conducted according to defined procedures.
- Defensibility: Conclusions reached through the process are supported by a rationale.
- Balance: Minority opinions and views of the person being reviewed are considered and recorded.
- Peer review activities are considered in the reappointment process.
- Conclusions from peer review are tracked over time.
- Actions based on conclusions are monitored for effectiveness.
- Findings, conclusions, recommendations, and actions are communicated to appropriate entities.
- Recommendations to improve performance are implemented.
- Physician leaders have a role in improving clinical processes used for clinical privileging.

As discussed in the section on credentialing and privileging, practitioner profiles are extremely important to maintain and are used to evaluate performance and maintain privileges. Some key aspects of these files include the following:

- Profiles are based on performance.
- Profiles are provided to each physician or provider on a regular basis.

- Organizations may use risk-adjusted software.
- Evidence-based medicine determines metrics used.
- Data are timely and accurate.
- Profiles are process focused.
- Physician data are grouped by specialty type or specific diagnoses.
- Data are reported regularly.
- Physician champions talk directly with medical staff about their data.

The physician data must be meaningful to physicians. They should represent major service lines and patient safety issues and include inpatient as well as outpatient data. When available, national targets and benchmarks are used to compare performance. For example, national rates of complications of certain procedures when compared with a specific physician or service can help the organization identify performance concerns about what is expected for the same procedure. The data are easily accessed and shared with the physician to improve performance, and the profiles vary according to the physician's specialty or area of practice. Some examples of elements that might be found in a physician profile can be found in the section on OPPE, such as

- patient volume,
- length of stay,
- average length of stay,
- DRGs,
- average cost per case,
- conformity with systemwide initiatives (e.g., use of deep vein thrombosis or pulmonary embolism prophylaxis),
- legibility of records,
- use of unapproved abbreviations,
- severity-adjusted mortality rate,
- severity-adjusted morbidity rate,
- death or loss of function related to HAI,
- unexpected transfers to ICU,
- unexpected death,
- unplanned return to surgery,
- procedure complications,
- charges for the patients treated by the physician compared with those for physicians in the same specialty,
- discharges,
- medication errors, and
- patient satisfaction (complaints or compliments).

Finally, these profiles are confidential, and there must be a mechanism to track activity when they are viewed. This might include a log or sign-out sheet (e.g., date of request, reason for request, name of person reviewing, and pertinent notes). Policies and procedures are needed to establish the system for document management. As for medical records, there must be defined mechanisms for how this information is shared or viewed.

J. Patient Advocacy

1. Recognition of Internal Customers

An important structural element in QPI is recognizing internal customers. Every process has both internal and external customers. Most people readily understand the concept of being a supplier of goods to an external customer. However, the idea of internal customers is equally important to QPI.

An employee can be a customer when she or he receives material, information, or services from others in the organization. Conversely, an employee also can be a supplier when she or he provides material, information, or services to others in the organization or to external customers. For example, when a nurse sends a specimen to the laboratory, the nurse is the supplier and the laboratory is the customer. When the laboratory sends a report back to the nurse, the laboratory is the supplier and the nurse is the customer. Just as there are suppliers to internal customers, those internal customers can, in turn, be suppliers to external customers. This approach can help to

- remind departments that do not have direct contact with external customers that they are still a critical link to customer satisfaction,
- improve relationships,
- make the work process flow smoothly, and
- avert potential bottlenecks.

Table 20 provides an example of an approach one organization followed to ensure the recognition of internal customers. Notice that the customer service standard pledge reflects the values necessary to make QPI a reality (e.g., teamwork, information sharing).

Table 20. Customer Service Standards and Pledge

Respect Me and My Job	**We Are All Professionals**	**Work and Communicate With Me**	**Smile—It's Contagious**
Our need: Respect. *Our response:* I understand the need to be respectful, and I will • acknowledge you, • be sensitive to your point of view, • thank you for a job well done, • value your time and priorities, • discuss my concerns with you in private, • value your job and its contribution to the organization, • treat you as I would like to be treated, and • speak to you in a pleasant tone in person or on the phone.	*Our need:* Professionalism. *Our response:* I understand the need to represent the hospital in a professional manner, and I will • take responsibility for my actions, • protect confidential information about patients and fellow employees, • look professional in dress, grooming, and manner, • coach others when necessary, and • follow through on my promise to you.	*Our need:* Teamwork. *Our response:* I understand the need for teamwork, and I will • pitch in and offer to help you whenever possible, • ask for your input before making a decision that may affect you, • talk to you directly instead of talking to others secretly if I have a concern, • listen to you, offer positive advice, and not interrupt until you are finished, • recognize that everyone has a valid opinion, and • seek out information and share what I have learned.	*Our need:* Positive attitude. *Our response:* I understand the need for a positive work environment, and I will • be sensitive to the effects my actions have on others, • replace criticism with positive ideas, • try to see things through the other person's eyes, • attempt to leave any personal problems at home, • coach my coworkers in portraying a positive attitude, and • project a caring and concerned attitude.

From Customer Service in Health Care: A Grassroots Approach to Creating a Culture of Service Excellence, *by K. Baird.*

In most healthcare organizations and as above, service excellence is as important as clinical excellence. For example, Sharp HealthCare (2012), a Malcolm Baldrige award recipient, has several initiatives that form the foundation of service excellence. These include

1. AIDET: Acknowledge, Introduce, Duration, Explanation, Thank you
2. Behavior standards:
   - Attitude is everything, create a lasting impression.
   - Thank somebody, reward and recognition.
   - Make words work, talk, listen and learn.
   - All for one, and one for all, teamwork.
   - Make it better, service recovery.
   - Think safe, be safe, safety at work.
   - Look Sharp-Be sharp, appearance speaks.
   - Keep in touch, ease waiting times.
   - It's a private matter, confidentiality.
   - To "E" or not to "E," e-mail manners.
   - Vive la difference! Diversity.
   - Get smart, increasing skills and competence.
3. Must haves:
   - Greet people with a smile and "Hello," using their name when possible.
   - Take people where they are going, rather than pointing or giving directions.
   - Use key words at key times: "Is there anything else I can do for you? I have the time."
   - Foster an attitude of gratitude. Send thank-you notes to deserving employees.
   - Round with reason to better connect with staff, patients, family, and other customers.
4. On Stage/Off Stage:
   This framework allows employees to stage patient and guest experiences, based on the premise that every action, object, and detail can either add to an experience or detract from it. Even small acts can be of great importance to patients and their families.
5. Storytelling:
   The development and sharing of stories can be a potent means or promoting values and beliefs in an organization. StoryCorps, a nonprofit organization, helps organizations "remind one another of our shared humanity, strengthen and build the connections between people, teach the value of listening, and weave into the fabric of our culture the understanding that every life matters" (StoryCorps, 2012, para. 2).

The measurement of customer perception, satisfaction, and loyalty is important for healthcare organizations to determine how their customers like the services provided. There are many vendors who survey these customers and provide data back to the organization for tracking, trending, and benchmarking performance.

The CMS has identified customer perception as a key component of measuring hospital performance and developed the Hospital Consumer Assessment of Healthcare Providers and Systems (HCAHPS; CMS, 2012) survey as a standardized method to compare performance and link payment to performance. The HCAHPS is the first national, standardized, publicly reported survey of patients' perspectives of hospital care. Before the advent of HCAHPS, there was no national standard for collecting and publicly reporting information about patient experience of care that allowed comparisons across hospitals locally, regionally, and nationally.

The survey is designed to produce data about patients' perceptions of care that allow objective comparisons of hospitals on topics that are important to consumers. Public reporting of the survey results increases accountability by increasing transparency in the quality of care. The CMS and the HCAHPS Project Team have taken steps to ensure the survey is credible, useful, and practical.

In 2002 CMS partnered with the AHRQ to develop and test the HCAHPS survey. In May 2005 the HCAHPS survey was endorsed by the NQF, and approval for the national implementation for public reporting occurred in March 2008. The survey, methods, and results are in the public domain.

The Deficit Reduction Act of 2005 created an additional incentive for acute care hospitals to participate in HCAHPS. As of July 2007, hospitals must collect and submit HCAHPS data to receive their full Inpatient Prospective Payment System annual payment update. Inpatient Prospective Payment System hospitals that fail to publicly report the HCAHPS survey may receive an annual payment update that is reduced by 2 percentage points. The Patient Protection and Affordable Care Act of 2010 (P.L. 111-148) includes HCAHPS among the measures to be used to calculate value-based incentive payments in the Hospital Value-Based Purchasing program, beginning with discharges in October 2012. HCAHPS results are published on the Hospital Compare website (www.hospitalcompare.hhs.gov) four times a year (www.hcahpsonline.org; CMS, n.d.). The survey consists of 27 questions with both inpatient and outpatient items depending on the population assessed.

Patient advocacy includes addressing the rights and responsibilities of patients and involving them in shared decision making, obtaining informed consent for treatment, and disclosing unanticipated outcomes. An advocate or ombudsman is often available to manage inquiries, requests, complaints, and grievances, with a process to document and track reported issues to resolution. An ethical framework is often applied with ethics consultation to respond to issues that may create conflict with the rights of the patient and the organization or others. The protection of the patients' rights may include a variety of concerns, such as

- abuse, neglect, and exploitation;
- financial responsibility;
- caregiving;
- decision-making ability and use of surrogates or durable power of attorney;
- advance directives or living wills;
- choices about healthcare and treatment;
- treatment without fear of retaliation; and
- visitation and support.

A recent change in patient rights is the inclusion of patients' responsibilities to actively engage in promoting health, decision making, and care as noted in **Figure 25**.

A patient's bill of rights was first adopted by the American Hospital Association in 1973. A revised version was approved in 1992 and is available on their website. More recently they have published the *Patient Care Partnership. Understanding Expectations, Rights and Responsibilities*, replacing the rights with a plain-language brochure.

Healthcare reform stresses an imperative to engage families in their own care. Enhancing patient-centered care that results in empowerment, engagement, and activation will become everyone's job. Patients and their families need to understand their role and responsibilities related to quality and safety. Patient-centered communication has been shown to improve clinical outcomes (Epstein & Street, 2007).

Figure 25. Patients' Bill of Rights and Responsibilities

I. Information Disclosure

You have the right to receive accurate and easily understood information about your health plan, healthcare professionals, and healthcare facilities. If you speak another language, have a physical or mental disability, or just don't understand something, assistance will be provided so you can make informed healthcare decisions.

II. Choice of Providers and Plans

You have the right to a choice of healthcare providers that is sufficient to provide you with access to appropriate, high-quality healthcare.

III. Access to Emergency Services

If you have severe pain, an injury, or sudden illness that convinces you that your health is in serious jeopardy, you have the right to receive screening and stabilization emergency services whenever and wherever needed, without prior authorization or financial penalty.

IV. Participation in Treatment Decisions

You have the right to know all your treatment options and to participate in decisions about your care. Parents, guardians, family members, or other individuals that you designate can represent you if you cannot make your own decisions.

V. Respect and Nondiscrimination

You have the right to considerate, respectful, and nondiscriminatory care from your doctors, health plan representatives, and other healthcare providers.

VI. Confidentiality of Health Information

You have the right to talk in confidence with healthcare providers and to have your healthcare information protected. You also have the right to review and copy your own medical record and request that your physician amend your record if it is not accurate, relevant, or complete.

VII. Complaints and Appeals

You have the right to a fair, fast, and objective review of any complaint you have against your health plan, doctors, hospitals, or other healthcare personnel. This includes complaints about waiting times, operating hours, the conduct of healthcare personnel, and the adequacy of healthcare facilities.

VIII. Consumer Responsibilities

Greater individual involvement by consumers in their care increases the likelihood of achieving the best outcomes and helps support a quality improvement, cost-conscious environment. Such responsibilities include

I. Take responsibility for maximizing healthy habits, such as exercising, not smoking, and eating a healthy diet.

II. Become involved in specific healthcare decisions.

III. Work collaboratively with healthcare providers in developing and carrying out agreed-upon treatment plans.

IV. Disclose relevant information and clearly communicate your wants and needs.

V. Use your health plan's internal complaint and appeal processes to address concerns that may arise.

VI. Avoid knowingly spreading disease.

VII. Recognize the reality of risks and limits of the science of medical care and the human fallibility of the healthcare professional.

VIII. Be aware of a healthcare provider's obligation to be reasonably efficient and equitable in providing care to other patients and the community.

IX. Become knowledgeable about your health plan coverage and health plan options (when available) including all covered benefits, limitations, and exclusions, rules regarding use of network providers, coverage and referral rules, appropriate processes to secure additional information, and the process to appeal coverage decisions.

X. Show respect for other patients and health workers.

XI. Make a good-faith effort to meet financial obligations.

XII. Abide by administrative and operational procedures of health plans, health care providers, and Government health benefit programs.

XIII. Report wrongdoing and fraud to appropriate resources or legal authorities.

From "Consumer Bill of Rights," in President's Advisory Commission on Consumer Protection and Quality in the Health Care Industry, *by the Agency for Healthcare Research and Quality, 1998. Available at www.hcqualitycommission.gov/cborr.*

Engagement is defined as "actions an individual must make to obtain the greatest benefit from the healthcare services available to them" (Center for Advancing Health, 2010, p. 2). Engaged patients produces better health outcomes (Von Korff, Gruman, Schaeffer, Curry, & Wagner, 1997; Kaplan, Greenfield, & Ware, 1989; Glascow, 2002). In this context, patient engagement involves an active process of synthesizing health information, recommendations of health care professionals, and personal beliefs and preferences to manage one's illness.

Various public and private entities have launched several initiatives to support consumer engagement. They are described below.

AHRQ: TalkingQuality. TalkingQuality is a comprehensive resource and guide for organizations that produce and disseminate reports to consumers on the quality of care healthcare organizations (e.g., hospitals, health plans, medical groups, nursing homes) and individual physicians provide. Consumer report sponsors share a common mission to improve the quality of care consumers receive. They also share a common challenge on how to convey comparative information about healthcare quality in a way that achieves the following objectives.

- Consumers are motivated to use it.
- Consumers can understand it.
- Consumers can apply the information to their own health care choices.

TalkingQuality was created to help you answer this question. It offers

- innovative ideas for communicating complex information on healthcare quality to consumers,
- information on the latest research findings, and
- real-world examples to illustrate various approaches and concepts.

While TalkingQuality focuses on the challenges and process of consumer reporting, much of the guidance applies equally well to organizations producing reports on healthcare quality to drive quality improvement and to inform other audiences, such as providers of care, payers, employers, and other stakeholders (AHRQ, n.d.).

AHRQ: Communication and Patient-Centered Care Toolkits. These toolkits contain resources to enhance communication between caregivers and patients.

- Improving Hospital Discharge Through Medication Reconciliation and Education,
- Improving Medication Adherence,
- Improving Medication Safety in Clinics for Patients 55 and Older,
- Improving Patient Safety Through Enhanced Provider Communication,
- Multidisciplinary Training for Medication Reconciliation,
- Reducing Discrepancies in Medication Orders and Histories at Handoffs,
- A Simulation-Based Safety Curriculum in a Children's Hospital ED,
- Testing the Re-engineered Hospital Discharge, and
- Using Military Simulation to Improve Rural Obstetric Safety,

AHRQ: Consumers and Patients. AHRQ has developed exceptional tools geared toward consumers and patients, providing "the latest evidence-based information for improving your health." "Getting Safer Care" includes resources in various forms, including written literature, podcasts, and videos.

Americans for Quality Health Care Quality Tool Box: Consumer Engagement. The National Partnership for Women and Families (NPWF) believe that "no single person, group or profession can improve health and healthcare throughout a community without the support of others" (NPWF, 2012).

The partnership has also developed a Consumer Partnership for e-Health. Tools have been developed for engaging consumers.

Patient-Centered Outcomes Research Institute (PCORI). According to it's website, PCORI "is an independent organization created to help people make informed healthcare decisions and improve healthcare delivery. PCORI will commission research that is guided by patients, caregivers, and the broader healthcare community and will produce high integrity, evidence-based information. PCORI is committed to transparency and a rigorous stakeholder-driven process that emphasizes patient engagement. PCORI will use a variety of forums and public comment periods to obtain public input throughout its work (PCORI, 2012, para. 1–2).

In March 2012, the PCORI Board refined its definition of patient-centered outcomes research. "Patient-centered outcomes research (PCOR) helps people and their caregivers communicate and make informed healthcare decisions, allowing their voices to be heard in assessing the value of healthcare options." This research answers patient-centered questions such as

1. Given my personal characteristics, conditions and preferences, what should I expect will happen to me?
2. What are my options and what are the potential benefits and harms of those options?
3. What can I do to improve the outcomes that are most important to me?
4. How can clinicians and the care delivery systems they work in help me make the best decisions about my health and healthcare? (PCORI, 2012)

PCORI has established national priorities for patient-centered comparative clinical effectiveness, which are

- Assessment of Prevention, Diagnosis, and Treatment Options: the research goal is to determine which option(s) work best for distinct populations with specific health problems;
- Improving Healthcare Systems: focuses on ways to improve healthcare services, such as the coordination of care for patients with multiple chronic conditions;
- Communication and Dissemination: looks at ways to provide information to patients so that they, in turn, can make informed healthcare decisions with clinicians;
- Addressing Disparities: assures that research addresses the healthcare needs of all patient populations. This is needed as treatments may not work equally well for everyone; and
- Accelerating Patient-Centered and Methodological Research: includes patients and caregivers in the design of research that is quick, safe, and efficient (PCORI, 2012).

Partnership for Patients. Partnership for Patients: Better Care, Lower Costs is a new public–private partnership that will help improve the quality, safety, and affordability of healthcare for all Americans. Using as much as $1 billion in new funding provided by the Affordable Care Act and leveraging a number of ongoing programs, the U.S. Department of Health and Human Services (HHS) will work with a wide variety of public and private partners to achieve the two core goals of this partnership—keeping patients from getting injured or sicker in the healthcare system and helping patients heal without complication by improving transitions from acute-care hospitals to other care settings, such as home or a skilled nursing facility. It's mission is to help patients "take care into their own hands."

Beyond reducing harm caused in hospitals, the Partnership for Patients is an important test of what can occur when the nation acts as one to address a major national health problem.

The recently formed Innovation Center at the Center for Medicare & Medicaid Services intends to dedicate over $500 million to test models of safer care delivery and promote implementation of best practices in patient safety. CMS will also provide $500 million for a

Community-Based Care Transition Program created by the Affordable Care Act to support hospitals and community-based organizations in helping Medicare beneficiaries at high risk for readmission to the hospital safely transition from the hospital to other care settings.

More than 7,300 partners, including more than 3,200 hospitals as well as physicians and nurses groups, consumer groups, and employers, have pledged their commitment to the Partnership for Patients (U.S. Department of Health and Human Services, 2011, para. 1–4).

K. Risk Management

"Risk management (RM) for healthcare entities can be defined as an organized effort to identify, assess, and reduce, where appropriate, risk to patients, visitors, staff and organizational assets" (Kavaler & Spiegel, 1997, p. 3). The goal of RM in any organization is to protect the organization from financial losses, which may arise because of the risks to which it is exposed. A healthcare risk manager must consider such things as regulatory compliance, safety management, credentialing, client–provider relations, publicity and media coverage, and, most importantly, patient care. In this way, RM and QPI are closely related. Both are keenly interested in maintaining or exceeding the applicable standard of care.

In the 1970s, RM was the initial reaction to continually increasing litigation. However, as litigation continued to rise, RM assumed a more proactive role in attempting to reduce the incidents of unsafe care. **Table 21** outlines the evolution of RM.

Risk management is the process of making and carrying out decisions that will minimize the adverse effects of accidental losses. The goal of RM is to protect the organization from financial loss, which may arise as a result of risks to which it is exposed. Whereas the traditional evolution demonstrates a strong focus on clinical RM, the concept of enterprise risk management is becoming more popular in expanding the focus of risks that affect the entire organization, not just the clinical operations. "Enterprise risk management (ERM) is a comprehensive business decision-making process instituted and supported by the healthcare organization's board, executive management, and medical staff leadership. ERM recognizes the synergistic effect of risks across the continuum of care, and has as its goals to reduce uncertainty and process variability, promote patient safety and maximize the return on investment (ROI) through asset preservation, and the recognition of actionable risk opportunities" (Carroll, 2010, p. 585). The major categories of risk in ERM include

- operational: risks related to the business operation that may result from failed processes, people, or systems (medical professional liability);
- financial: risks that affect the profitability, cash flow access to capital, or financial ratings;
- human capital: risks associated with a tight labor market, including selection, retention, and compensation;
- strategic: brand and reputational risks associated with business strategy, changing priorities, and competition;
- legal and regulatory: risks associated with licensure, accreditation, product liability, and intellectual property issues;
- technology: risks associated with machines, equipment, devices, hardware, and software; and
- hazard: risks related to physical loss of assets, often associated with natural hazards.

1. Risk Identification

Risk identification is the first step to determine what risks can affect the achievement of organizational goals. Both formal and informal methods are used, and the risks may be internal or external to the organization. Approaches used include retrospective, concurrent,

Table 21. Evolution of Healthcare Risk Management

Number one goal: protect financial resources and reputation.	Number one goal: improve patient safety and minimize risk of harm to patient through better understanding of systemic factors that limit caregiver's ability to provide safe care.
Paper occurrence form required.	Variety of methods to report: paper form, electronic form, telephone call, anonymous reporting, person-to-person reporting.
Investigate only the serious occurrences.	Encourage reporting of "near misses," and investigate and discuss the potential root causes.
Interview staff one on one when there is an adverse incident.	Have root cause analysis meetings with the entire team of caregivers. Identify system factors that contributed to the event.
Information from investigation kept confidential.	Develop corrective action, share with patient safety committee and others in the organization.
Blame and train.	Perform a criticality analysis chart and determine the root cause of the "near miss" or the adverse occurrence.
Talk to the patient or patient's family only if necessary and be vague about findings.	Advise physician to speak directly with the patient or family and talk with them about any unexpected outcomes and errors; keep them apprised of steps taken to make environment safe for next patient.
Work with department involved to develop corrective action.	Work with team to develop a patient safety improvement plan.
Assume that action is taken to correct the problem that occurred, notice only when it happens again that no action was taken.	Monitor the patient safety improvement plan to determine that changes have been initiated and that the changes have made a difference.
Keep patients in the dark about risk management and occurrence reporting.	Establish ongoing patient safety education; publish patient safety bulletins that address specific patient safety issues and the organization's approach to managing them; provide opportunity for patients to identify methods of improving patient safety and to share them with administration.

From "The need for risk management to evolve to assure a culture of safety," by A. M. Kuhn, & B. J. Youngberg, 2002, Quality and Safety in Health Care, 11, pp. 158–162. Copyright 2002 by Quality and Safety in Health Care, BMJ Publishing Group. Reprinted with permission.

pre-interventional, and prospective. Once the risks have been identified, the next step is to conduct a risk assessment to quantify the magnitude or severity of the risks, the exposure through possible results, frequency of occurrence, probability of the occurrence, and time to act. Through this analysis, the organization can determine RM techniques that can be applied to the exposures to mitigate loss, select the best RM technique for the situation, prioritize actions, identify resources needed, identify risk control and risk financing methods, implement the techniques, monitor the effectiveness of the technique, and trend and analyze results. **Table 22** shows domains and measures to be considered for possible clinical risk areas based on the NQF's *Consensus Standards for Quality of Hospital Care.*

2. Risk Evaluation and Prevention

The enterprise risk manager is an important asset to the organization, as that person is charged with risk identification, risk assessment and evaluation, and application of techniques to reduce risks. Duties vary widely by organization, but the basic enterprise RM functions are

- risk identification, assessment, planning, mitigation, and evaluation;
- maintenance and monitoring of effective incident reporting and occurrence screen programs;

- claim management;
- clinical and administrative responsibilities such as policy review, credentialing, contract review, internal and external reporting, and education;
- collaboration and communication with safety officer, patient safety officer, and quality management;
- collaboration with the financial officer on insurance and other risk financing methods;
- collaboration and communication with legal representatives for claim management; and
- regulatory compliance.

Table 22. National Quality Forum Consensus Standards for Quality of Hospital Care

Domain	Measure
Length of stay and readmission	Risk-adjusted average length of inpatient hospital stay
	Overall inpatient hospital average length of stay (ALOS) and ALOS by diagnosis-related group (DRG) service category
	All-cause readmission index
	30-day all-cause risk standardized readmission rate following heart failure hospitalization
	Severity: standardized ALOS—routine care
	Severity: standardized ALOS—special care
	Severity: standardized ALOS—deliveries
Patient safety, adult	Accidental puncture or laceration
	Death in low-mortality DRGs
	Iatrogenic pneumothorax
	Death among surgical inpatients with serious, treatable complications
	Bilateral cardiac catheterization rate
	Blood cultures performed within 24 hours before or 24 hours after hospital arrival for patients who were transferred or admitted to intensive care unit (ICU) within 24 hours of hospital arrival
	Congestive heart failure mortality
	Hip fracture mortality rate
	Transfusion reaction, age 18 years and older
Domain	**Measure**
Patient safety, pediatrics	Accidental puncture or laceration
	Decubitus ulcer
	Iatrogenic pneumothorax in nonneonates
	Transfusion reaction, age under 18 years
Pediatrics	Pediatric ICU (PICU) severity-adjusted length of stay
	PICU unplanned readmission rate
	Review of unplanned PICU readmissions
	Home management plan-of-care document given to patient or caregiver
	Pediatric heart surgery mortality
	Pediatric heart surgery volume
	PICU pain assessment on admission
	PICU periodic pain assessment
	PICU standardized mortality ratio

(continued)

Table 22. National Quality Forum: Consensus Standards for Quality of Hospital Care *(continued)*

Surgery and anesthesia	Abdominal aortic aneurysm volume
	Abdominal aortic aneurysm repair mortality rate
	Esophageal resection mortality rate
	Esophageal resection volume
	Incidental appendectomy in the elderly rate
	Pancreatic resection mortality rate
	Pancreatic resection volume
	Postoperative wound dehiscence, age under 18 years
	Postoperative wound dehiscence, age 18 years and older
	Foreign body left after procedure, age under 18 years
	Foreign body left in during procedure, 18 years and older
	Failure to rescue—in-hospital mortality
	Failure to rescue—30-day mortality
Venous thrombo-embolism (VTE)	VTE prophylaxis
	ICU VTE prophylaxis
	VTE patients with anticoagulation overlap therapy
	VTE patients—unfractionated heparin dosages/platelet count monitoring by protocol (or nomogram)
	VTE discharge instructions
	Incidence of potentially preventable VTE

From "National Quality Forum Endorses Consensus Standards for Quality of Hospital Care: Patient Safety in Hospitals Focus of 48 NQF-Endorsed Measures." Retrieved from www.qualityforum.org/Projects/h/Hospital_Care_Performance_(2002)/Hospital_Care__Performance_Evaluation_Framework.aspx. Copyright 2012 by National Quality Forum. Reprinted with permission.

Risk Management Plan. A healthcare organization typically has a plan explaining its enterprise RM philosophy. Often the enterprise RM plan is integrated with the quality management plan because the two processes are interdependent. Important plan elements include

- purpose and board statement of support of enterprise RM;
- scope of the program, authority, and confidentiality assertions;
- data collection and reporting mechanisms (both internal and external); and
- integration with quality management and program effectiveness reviews.

Within the plan, prevention of risk is often managed with

- contract review,
- internal and external reporting processes,
- education of staff and providers,
- policy review to protect the organization, and
- informed consent.

Usually risk control is managed through incident (or variance) reporting, occurrence screening, and claim management. The data that may be useful when trended or analyzed include

- liability claims,
- workers' compensation claims,
- physical malpractice coverage,

- incident reports,
- occurrence screens,
  - review of records using criteria to note variations,
  - details of the occurrence,
  - records that need more in-depth review,
  - confirmation of the variation or absence of an untoward event, and
  - summary of data with trends
- patient complaints, and
- tort claims.

Possible causes of losses for organizations include

- criminal acts by employees;
- breach of contract;
- patient harm related to inability of contractors to perform services;
- clinical treatment by qualified or unqualified staff;
- improper use of equipment by staff, patients, or families;
- inappropriate discharge;
- falls with injury;
- medication errors with harm;
- lack of informed consent;
- privacy violations;
- problems with employer–employee relations;
- failure to meet licensing laws or regulations;
- antitrust issues; and
- Medicare or Medicaid fraud.

An important aspect of enterprise RM is management of claims. **Figure 26** lists the types of professional liability sources often considered in determining the validity of a claim, and **Figure 27** shows the key elements for a tort.

Figure 26. Professional Liability Sources

Corporate liability	Based on recognition that the organization owes a duty to the patients it serves
Vicarious liability	Indirect responsibility for the acts of another person; *respondeat superior,* which holds the employer responsible for the wrongful acts of its employees
Ostensible agency	Generally an organization is not liable for injuries sustained by patients because of the actions of an independent contractor. However, the extension of *respondeat superior* to the doctrine of the ostensible agency may extend liability exposure to the organization for acts of nonemployed, independent contractor physicians where no employer–employee relationship exists.
Res ipsa loquitur	Allows a patient to prove his or her case without needing to establish the standard of care in which there is clear and obvious negligence.

Figure 27. Elements for a Tort

Duty	Harm or injury as a result of the breach
Breach of duty	Causation

Education and Skills for Risk Managers. It is helpful for risk managers to have some clinical knowledge, because they must review care and provide guidance to clinical providers of care. Because risk managers must review defense counsel work and legal documents, they should have some knowledge of healthcare law and have a thorough understanding of the legal system. Finally, understanding the insurance industry is important because risk managers help make decisions about various insurance coverages such as hospital professional liability, general liability, and workers' compensation.

L. Organizational QPI Training

Everyone in the organization is responsible for quality and safety. Therefore, educating all employees at all levels of the organization is critical to the success of QPI. Because the most common cause of failure in any QPI effort is uninvolved or indifferent top and middle management, it is essential that all leaders be educated from the start. Training should begin at the top and cascade down through the organization. Ultimately, senior and middle management should be part of the teaching team; this will demonstrate to employees that they are committed to QPI. The method of education or training must be tailored to the audience and use tools and methods to match the audience needs and learning styles. Governing body or board members must also be included in understanding QPI and their accountability for quality of care in the organization. Some form of board training is often included for new members. A comprehensive program for all levels of employees, management, board, and physicians should be designed to meet the needs of these different groups. For example, governing-board training should include a review of oversight responsibility for the organization's quality and safety performance, some form of quality and safety committee or review function, use of quality performance as a criterion in rating executive performance, and trends and public reporting of the organization's data and its image in the community.

1. Determining Education and Training Needs

There are many ways to determine the educational needs of QPI participants (Gaucher & Coffey, 1993; Kirkpatrick, 1998; Phillips & Stone, 2002). Methods to obtain information should include

- evaluating knowledge and skills contained in the job description,
- asking participants,
- asking participants' supervisors,
- asking others who are knowledgeable about the job (e.g., customer, peers, experts in QPI),
- testing participants on their skills and knowledge, and
- analyzing participants' past performance appraisals.

2. Fundamentals of QPI Curriculum

The curriculum should include the following elements:

- explanation of the need for organizational improvement, including individual and collective benefits of QPI;
- development and use of common quality language or taxonomy;
- discussion of the organization's QPI goals;
- definition of the QPI structure;
- articulation of QPI philosophy and a model for improvement;
- description of the QPI process;
- description and clarification of responsibilities;
- tools and techniques to participate in teams and to manage work processes;

- description of how change may affect the individual's job and work relationships;
- metrics for the organization; and
- reporting structure for leaders and staff.

Training should be tailored to the specific needs of each group (i.e., top management, middle management, front-line staff). **Table 23** offers a comparison of topics addressed across major groups in a QPI curriculum. Another approach to considering training is the Institute for Healthcare Improvement (IHI) Improvement Advisor Professional Development Program (IHI, n.d.), which includes the following agenda for training:

- science of improvement (includes high reliability organizations),
- model for improvement,
- scoping improvement efforts,
- understanding systems and processes,
- using data for improvement,
- understanding relationships,
- gathering information,
- organizing information,
- developing powerful ideas for change,
- testing changes,
- implementing changes,
- decision making,

Table 23. Suggested Substantive Issues for QPI Education and Training

Quality as a strategic advantage	Key concepts of quality and performance management (e.g., customer satisfaction, process management, teamwork, continuous improvement methods)	Quality awareness, definition of quality
Role of leadership in creating and sustaining quality vision	Principles of customer service	Quality participation: fundamental training in QPI, including process improvement tools and techniques
Integrating quality values into day-to-day leadership	Managing process performance (measurement, QPI tools, variation, problem solving, data collection and analysis)	Organization's mission, vision, and QPI plan
Indicators for measuring and evaluating quality and organizational performance	Measurement of quality outcomes	Concepts of quality management: customer satisfaction, process improvement, teamwork, continuous improvement
Components of quality management implementation process	Management practices for building teamwork, employee involvement and recognition for customer service, team contributions for quality, team leadership skills, conflict resolution, communication skills, listening and giving feedback, accreditation standards	Promoting cooperation between coworkers within and between departments
Basic QPI tools		Communication skills
Role as team leaders		Customer service
Awareness of accreditation standards		Relevant standards

- working with people, and
- planned experimentation.

3. What Skills Do Healthcare Quality Professionals Need?

The key operating assumption of building capacity is that different groups of people will have different levels of need for QPI knowledge and skills. A teaching plan should ensure that each group receives the knowledge and skill sets they need, when they need them, and in the appropriate amounts. **Figure 28** shows a pyramid model in which experts need a high level of specific knowledge on performance improvement, quality management, and tools, whereas most staff need a much lower level of knowledge in this area.

The potential audience for QPI training includes experts, executives or top management, middle management, and staff. Training topics for these groups can be classified as follows:

Top management education topics:

- quality and safety as strategic advantages;
- role of leadership in sustaining quality vision;
- integration of quality and safety culture and values;
- indicators for measuring and evaluating;
- components of QPI implementation process;
- basic QPI tools;
- role as team leaders, champions, and sponsors; and
- awareness of accreditation and regulatory standards.

Middle management education topics:

- QPI key concepts;
- customer service principles;
- management of process performance;
- measurement of quality and safety outcomes; and
- management practices regarding teams, conflict resolution, communication skills, regulations, and accreditation standards.

Staff (what everyone should know) education topics:

- QPI awareness: definition of quality;
- fundamental QPI training;

Figure 28. Levels of Knowledge

High Level of Knowledge

Low Level of Knowledge

- organization's mission, vision, and QPI plan;
- concepts of QPI: customer satisfaction, process improvement, teamwork, and continuous improvement;
- promotion of cooperation between coworkers for cross-functional or interdisciplinary teams;
- communication skills;
- customer service;
- just-in-time team training; and
- relevant standards.

There are some common reasons why managers are often reluctant to support training in this area. These barriers must be overcome for the organization to develop the infrastructure necessary to support healthcare quality and safety. They include

- no results from the training;
- too costly;
- no input on the content, process, or timing;
- no relevance of the content to actual work;
- no involvement in the process;
- no time for staff to participate;
- lack of preparation of programs;
- lack of knowledge about learning and development; and
- no requirements for the training (e.g., no regulations; Phillips & Phillips, 2003, pp. 2–4).

M. Training on QPI, Program Development, and Evaluation

Providing the training on QPI is often a collaborative effort between healthcare quality professionals as the subject matter experts and educators as the experts on teaching and learning modalities. There are multiple approaches to education using adult learning principles and accelerated learning methods, including the following:

- Engage multiple senses to enhance learning (auditory, visual, kinesthetic).
- Use concepts and principles, then add application into practice.
- Allow "toys" to activate the brain to facilitate learning.
- Allow students to teach each other key concepts; acting as a teacher promotes a stronger focus on learning.
- Chunk learning material into key categories and teach in segments, building on easier concepts and then adding more difficult ones.

The use of simulation and case studies to apply concepts or tools is another effective way to enhance training. Most types of hands-on experience and practice will make the learning fun and more relevant and increase muscle memory for the task.

Training on QPI must address the current employee base, new employees, and ongoing processes. Although core concepts and tools can be taught and reemphasized to embed the improvement philosophy into the culture, there will be degradation in memory unless the information is clearly integrated into daily work and used often. For this reason, just-in-time training is often used for teams or projects.

New tools and techniques are continuously added to the toolbox for employees so that advanced data management and analysis can be performed. This accumulation supports the concepts of a learning organization, as described by both Senge and Garvin. Senge (1990) first described the key components of a learning organization: systems thinking, personal mastery, mental models, shared vision, and team learning.

Senge also described the benefits of a learning organization:

- maintaining levels of innovation and remaining competitive,
- learning to respond to external pressures,
- learning to link resources to customer needs,
- improving quality at all levels,
- improving organizational image, and
- increasing the pace of change in the organization.

According to Garvin, three issues must be addressed before an organization can become a learning organization (Garvin, 1993). He defined *learning organization* in this way: "A learning organization is an organization skilled at creating, acquiring and transferring knowledge and at modifying its behavior to reflect new knowledge and insights" (Garvin, 1993, p. 80). The three areas that must be addressed by leadership are meaning, management, and measurement. Although he describes five components of the learning organization, they differ slightly from Senge's description. He states that an organization must be skilled at five key activities:

- systematic problem solving,
- experimentation with new approaches,
- learning from past experience,
- learning from best practices, and
- transferring knowledge quickly and efficiently throughout the organization.

By building a learning organization, leaders foster an environment conducive to learning. This opens up boundaries across departments, disciplines, and professions and stimulates the exchange of ideas. The way to foster this development is to create learning forums, which may take many forms to achieve innovation and learning. The learning organization will excel in a culture of performance excellence and improvement because the cultural foundation will support ongoing learning, change, and improvement.

N. Effectiveness Evaluation of QPI Training

Kirkpatrick's foundational principles for evaluating effectiveness of training were first published in 1959. The focus was a return on expectations as the ultimate indicator of value, and value must be created before it can be measured. The framework for evaluation can be envisioned as a compelling chain of evidence that demonstrates the bottom-line value to the organization (**Figure 29**).

1. Framework for Evaluating the Results of Training

As an expert in the field of training, Donald Kirkpatrick (1998) perceived three reasons for evaluating training programs:

- to determine how to improve future training,
- to determine whether the current training should be continued, and
- to justify the existence of the training department.

To the extent trainers can demonstrate important outcomes from training, they will be seen as important to the QPI movement and the organization itself. Kirkpatrick (1998) suggests there are four important levels of training evaluation: reaction, learning, behavior, and results. This model is often used to describe various levels of measuring training effectiveness.

Figure 29. Framework Linkage

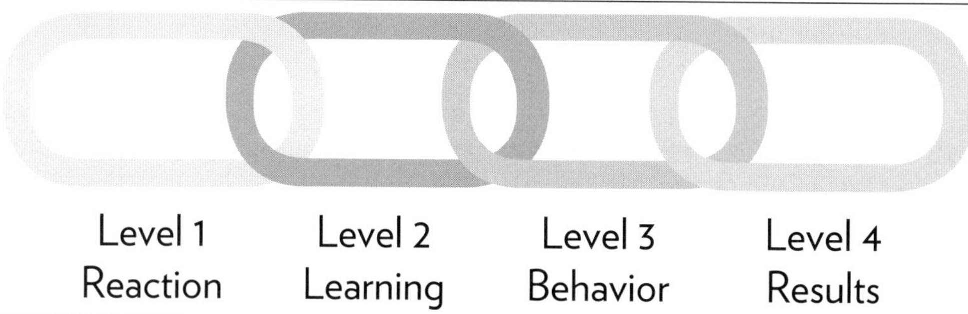

From The Kirkpatrick Model. Retrieved from www.kirkpatrickpartners.com/OurPhilosophy/tabid/66/Default.aspx. Copyright 2011 by Kirkpatrick Partners. Reprinted with permission.

Reaction. This is the extent to which the participants are satisfied with training. Because negative attitudes toward the program can interfere with learning, this is an important measurement. Reactions are often measured at the end of the training program or soon after the program has ended through use of a questionnaire about what participants thought and felt about the training. For example, here are two ways of measuring reactions:

- Customer (trainee) satisfaction, or their opinion (What did they like? What did they learn? Was anything missing?), using a Likert rating scale for feedback.
- Good facilitator, interesting or useful subject, adequate facilities, opinion of atmosphere, scheduling, additional comments.

Learning. When participants change attitudes, improve knowledge, or increase skill as a result of the program, learning has occurred. Unless one of these parameters has changed, it is unlikely that behavior will change. Learning is best measured both before and after training and, where possible, should include some type of control group as a basis of comparison. The type of measure used will depend on what is being evaluated. For example, increased skill may need to be evaluated by a specialist in that particular area, whereas a change in attitude can be measured using a before-and-after questionnaire. For example, learning can be measured by a change in attitude, skills, or knowledge and using pre- and posttests, test performance, demonstrations, or role play.

Behavior. This level refers to behavioral change as a result of training. It focuses on the transfer of knowledge, skills, or attitudes from the classroom to the job. Although positive reactions may produce a desire to change behavior, and learning may give participants the skills to know how and what to change, it does not necessarily follow that behavior will actually change. In addition to positive reactions and learning, employees must work in a climate supportive of change, and they must see some reward associated with changing their behaviors. This does not have to be tangible rewards; intangible rewards such as a feeling of achievement also are important motivators for change. The climate depends heavily on the support of the supervisor, further supporting the importance of all levels of management being involved in QPI education and training. Ideally, behaviors are measured both before and after training, allowing ample time for behavioral change to occur. Pretraining and posttraining information can be collected in the form of questionnaires and interviews and should be elicited from participants and from those who are in a position to observe participants' behaviors (e.g., immediate supervisor, customers, peers). Some relevant examples of behavioral changes relating to QPI may include the extent to which

- department heads deploy QPI concepts, methods, and tools;
- senior leaders communicate the organization's values (measured by employee questionnaires and focus groups); and
- leadership practices reflect employee involvement and participation.

Results. This is the last—and probably the most important—level of program evaluation described by Kirkpatrick. Indicators used to measure results should be tied to the driving force behind conducting training in the first place. For example, did quality of care actually improve, and was this a function of QPI training? Were overall errors reduced through organization-wide QPI training? As with evaluation of behavioral changes, result evaluation should be conducted before and after training, use a control group, allow ample time for results to be achieved, monitor results over time, and compare the cost of the training program with the benefit. In some cases, a direct link between training and results will be difficult to prove because many other factors might influence a particular outcome. However, evidence that supports the link should be gathered. Examples of results may include

- final overall change for the business as a result of the training program;
- improved quality, improved production, or decreased costs; and
- increased job satisfaction, reduced problems or accidents, or increased sales.

Return on Investment. J. J. Phillips has suggested a fifth level of evaluation: ROI evaluation, in which the fourth level of the standard model is compared with the overall costs of training (Phillips, 1996; Phillips & Phillips, 2005). The ROI evaluation addresses how the bottom line changed as a result of training. The ROI asks the question "Were the benefits greater than the cost?" (Phillips, 1996). Phillips describes methods for isolating the effects of the program or process, methods of converting data to monetary values, cost categories, intangible benefits, and communication targets.

2. Aligning Rewards to Support Quality

Reward systems are critical to the success of QPI. In fact, "The most damaging alignment problem to which many total quality failures have been attributed is the lack of alignment between expectations that arise from total quality change processes and reward systems" (Evans & Dean, 2003, p. 362). Rewards are important because they can motivate people. Motivating people to provide excellent customer service is a top priority for most organizations. Therefore, before discussing rewards, it is important to understand motivation.

a. Basics of Motivation

Work motivation is "the psychological forces that determine the *direction* of a person's behavior in an organization, a person's level of *effort*, and a person's level of *persistence*" (George & Jones, 2002, p. 181). There are many theories of motivation, and each has somewhat different but complementary implications for actions managers can take to motivate employees. Therefore, a basic understanding of all the major theories is important. One way to view all theories is through the "motivation equation" (George & Jones, 2002). Each theory stresses different parts of the equation (**Figure 30**).

1.) Need Theories

Need theories center on what employees are motivated to obtain from work (outcomes). These theories include Maslow's hierarchy of needs, McClelland's need theory, and Hertzberg's two-factor theory.

Abraham H. Maslow's (1954) need theory was first published in 1943. Maslow, a psychologist, believed that human needs could be arranged in a hierarchy from the most basic to higher order needs, as follows:

Figure 30. Motivation Equation

Need Theory

What *outcomes* are individuals motivated to obtain in the workplace?

Expectancy Theory

Do individuals believe that their *inputs* will result in a given level of *performance*?

Do individuals believe that *performance* at this level will lead to obtaining *outcomes* they desire?

Equity Theory

Are *outcomes* perceived as being at an appropriate level in comparison with *inputs*?

Procedural Justice

Are the *procedures* used to assess inputs and performance and to distribute outcomes perceived as fair?

From Organizational Behavior, *by J.M. George & G.R. Jones, 2002, Upper Saddle River, NJ: Prentice Hall. Copyright 2002 by Prentice Hall. Reprinted with permission.*

- physiological or survival needs (basic survival needs such as food and water),
- safety or security needs (protection from harm or physical deprivation),
- belongingness or social needs (the need for interaction with others, companionship, belonging, and friendship),
- esteem or status needs (needs for recognition and appreciation), and
- self-actualization needs (the need for self-fulfillment or to reach one's highest potential).

Maslow believed that basic needs had to be met before higher order needs. For example, employees would have to meet basic survival needs (e.g., working in a safe environment) before they would focus on esteem needs. In addition, Maslow maintained that only unsatisfied needs served to motivate people; people want what they do not have.

David C. McClelland proposed a concept similar to Maslow's, narrowing the number of needs to three types: achievement, power, and affiliation (McClelland, Atkinson, Clark, & Lowell, 1976).

Finally, Frederick Herzberg's two-factor theory classified the elements of motivation into two categories: motivators and hygiene factors (Herzberg, Maysner, & Snyderman, 1966). Motivators are the elements of a job that increase job satisfaction, including challenging work, achievement, recognition, growth, and advancement. Hygiene factors, on the other hand, do not contribute to motivation, but their absence leads to dissatisfaction. Hygiene factors include company policy and administrative issues such as supervision, working conditions, interpersonal relations, safety, salaries, morale, and productivity. Herzberg expanded on Maslow's theory, making a distinction between factors that motivate and factors that maintain motivation.

At least two managerial implications for motivation are clear from need theories:

- There are many different needs, and these differ between employees.
- If employees are not motivated, managers should seek to determine what needs employees have and which are satisfied or unsatisfied.

2.) Expectancy Theory

Expectancy theory is concerned with how people decide which behaviors to engage in and how much effort they should give to that behavior. This theory focuses on the person's perception of effort-to-performance and performance-to-outcome links. Essentially, a person asks himself or herself, "If I work hard (effort), will I be able to perform?" Motivation is improved by strengthening that link. Managers want to be certain that employees believe that if they work hard, they will achieve high performance. Thus, providing training and education so that they have the appropriate skills to perform the work would improve motivation.

Individuals also ask themselves, "If I perform at a high level, will there be an outcome, and is it something I care about?" To strengthen this performance-outcome link, managers want employees to believe that if they perform at a high level, there will be an outcome that they desire. Managers can strengthen this link by having valid performance appraisal systems that capture quality performance and also by having systems in place to reward such performance. For example, when an employee reports an adverse event, there should be an immediate outcome that is positive in the eyes of that employee.

In accordance with this theory, managers should do the following:

- Be certain employees have the necessary skills to perform well.
- Coach employees to believe that if they work hard they will be successful.
- Know what outcomes employees perceive as important (as detailed by needs theory).
- Have clear policies about what levels of performance are rewarded (result in outcomes) and which levels are not.

3.) Equity Theory

Equity theory centers on the input and outcomes part of the motivation equation. The overall idea is that employees are motivated when there is fairness in the workplace. This theory contends that employees determine fairness by looking at the ratio of their inputs (work effort) to their outcomes (e.g., rewards, benefits). For example, Employee A may be motivated if she receives a financial bonus that she perceives to be equitable given her effort on the QPI project. According to this theory, however, employees also compare the ratio of their inputs to outcomes with those of others' inputs and outcomes. Therefore, if Employee B in the same department is awarded a larger financial bonus for the same amount of effort, Employee A's motivation would probably drop. Some ways for managers to motivate employees include the following:

- Acknowledge different performance levels with different levels of rewards.
- Periodically check employees' perceptions about their own input and outcomes as well as those of others.
- Know what outcomes are desirable and tie those to performance in a timely manner.

4.) Procedural Justice

Procedural justice is a theory of motivation that focuses on fairness with respect to processes or procedures used to allocate outcomes. Research has demonstrated that people are more likely to see outcome allocations as fair when the following conditions exist:

- Employees have input into how decisions are made.
- There is an opportunity for performance errors to be corrected.
- Rules and policies for allocation of outcomes are applied consistently.
- Decisions are made in an unbiased manner.

b. What Do Employees Say?

There is research support for these various motivation theories. In the past 25 years, the Gallup Organization undertook two extremely large studies. The first asked, "What do the most talented employees need from their workplace?" For this part of the research, Gallup interviewed more than 1 million people who were employed across a broad range of companies, industries, and countries. This study's "most powerful" conclusion is that the retention and performance of an employee is determined "by his relationship with his immediate supervisor" (Buckingham & Coffman, 1999). So what makes a good supervisor? Gallup's data indicate that there are 12 factors critical to the retention and performance of employees:

- Do I know what is expected of me at work?
- Do I have the materials and equipment I need to do my work correctly?
- Do I have the opportunity at work to do what I do best every day?
- In the last 7 days, have I received recognition or praise for doing good work?
- Does my supervisor, or someone at work, seem to care about me as a person?
- Is there someone at work who encourages my development?
- Do my opinions seem to count at work?
- Does the mission or purpose of my work organization make me feel my job is important?
- Are my coworkers committed to doing high-quality work?
- Do I have a best friend at work?
- In the last 6 months, has someone at work talked to me about my progress?
- This past year, have I had opportunities at work to learn and grow?

These factors clearly are consistent with the theories of motivation discussed previously.

3. Setting Up a Reward System

Given the role rewards play in employee motivation, setting up an effective reward system is important. Seven steps are fundamental to a reward system (Gaucher & Coffey, 1993):

- Determine priorities and values; behaviors that will be rewarded are prioritized.
- Identify the criteria or milestones.
- Establish a budget for recognition.
- Determine who will be accountable for managing the recognition.
- Develop specific procedures and features of the rewards and recognition.
- Obtain feedback from employees on desired rewards and recognition.
- Modify program based on feedback.

The most important step is to reward the desired behavior.

O. Communicating Successes

Sharing organization success stories internally and externally is important for several reasons. As described earlier, it motivates employees and serves as both reward and recognition to them. The value is demonstrated to the employees in increasing knowledge transfer, learning from experience, sharing best practices, and stimulating innovation within the organization. Value is next demonstrated to the customer in showcasing successful processes and outcomes to the people served. Communicating successes also demonstrates accountability and transparency to the community and public served. There may be other stakeholders for whom communicating success is also important. Externally, sharing of lessons learned with other organizations, professional groups, online communities, and the public might be performed in different ways. Some of the more common groups for sharing are professional conferences, committees, and professional organizations. The report format often includes

- abstract,
- title,
- objectives,
- outline,
- content,
- results, and
- references.

The form in which communication takes place can also include face-to-face presentations, webinars, posters and storyboards, publications, and social networking tools. Publications may be local newsletters, peer-reviewed journals, or online forums including blogs. It is necessary to follow specific submission guidelines for a poster, abstract, or article. The publishing organization will define poster measurements, labeling design, and key elements for text and graphics. Abstract criteria will focus on topics of interest, maximum and minimum word limits, and categories to include. Journal articles must conform to author guidelines and use a specific writing style. In preparing to use any of these external communication methods, it is essential to have samples of work product reviewed to increase the chances of acceptance.

VI. Summary

A formal QPI program and infrastructure is required to ensure quality and safety. The tenets of quality and safety must first be developed through strategic planning. In this book, a discussion of strategic planning is followed by the establishment of priorities for QPI activities, translating strategic goals into quality outcomes, and aligning culture and structure to support QPI. QPI teams are described, as are patient advocacy, risk management, and training.

Through the understanding of QPI principles reviewed herein and in other *Q Solutions* products, the healthcare quality professional can apply evidence-based techniques to ensure quality and safety in their healthcare organizations.

References

Agency for Healthcare Research and Quality. (n.d.). About TeamSTEPPS. Retrieved from http://teamstepps.ahrq.gov/about-2cl_3.htm

Agency for Healthcare Research and Quality. (2012). About TalkingQuality. Retrieved from www.ahrq.gov/talkingquality/about.htm

American Combatives, Inc. (2009). *Airline crew safety training program*. Retrieved from www.americancombatives.com/index.php?option=com_content&view=article&id=66&Itemid=79

American Hospital Association. (1999). *Accountability: The pathway to restoring public trust and confidence for hospitals and other healthcare organizations*. Retrieved from www.aha.org/content/00-10/AHAPrinciplesAccountability.pdf

Baird, K. (2000). *Customer service in health care: A grassroots approach to creating a culture of service excellence*. San Francisco, CA: Jossey-Bass.

Baldrige Performance Excellence Program. (2011–2012). *Health care criteria for performance excellence*. Retrieved from www.nist.gov/baldrige/publications/hc_criteria.cfm

Begun, J., Zimmerman, B., & Dooley, K. (2003). Health care organizations as complex adaptive systems. In S. Mick & M. Wyttenbach (Eds.), *Advances in health care organization theory* (pp. 253–258). San Francisco, CA: Jossey-Bass.

Berwick, D. M., & Hackbarth, A. D. (2012). Eliminating waste in US health care. *JAMA, 307*(14), 1513–1516. doi:10.1001/jama.2012.362

Buckingham, M., & Coffman, C. (1999). *First, break all the rules: What the world's greatest managers do differently*. New York, NY: Simon & Schuster.

Byers, J. F., & Beaudin, C. L. (2001). Critical appraisal tools facilitate the work of the quality professional. *Journal for Healthcare Quality, 23*(5), 35–38, 40–43. doi:10.1111/j.1945-1474.2001.tb00374.x

Byers, J. F., & Beaudin, C. L. (2002). The relationship between continuous quality improvement and research. *Journal for Healthcare Quality, 24*(1), 4–8.

Campion, M. A., Medsker, G. J., & Higgs, C. A. (1993). Relations between work group characteristics and effectiveness: Implications for designing effective work groups. *Personnel Psychology, 46*, 823–850. doi:10.1111/j.1744-6570.1993.tb01571.x

Carroll, R. (Ed.). (2010). *Risk management handbook for healthcare organizations*, (student ed.). San Francisco: Jossey Bass.

Center for Advancing Health. (2010). *A new definition of patient engagement: What is engagement and why is it important?* Washington, DC: Author.

Centers for Disease Control and Prevention. (2011). SMART objectives template. Retrieved from www.cdc.gov/phcommunities/docs/Evaluate_SMART_Objectives_Template.doc

Centers for Medicare & Medicaid Services. (n.d.). *HCAHPS: Hospital care quality information from the consumer perspective*. Retrieved from www.hcahpsonline.org

Centers for Medicare & Medicaid Services. (2012). *HCAHPS: Patients' perspective of care survey*. Retrieved from www.cms.gov/HospitalQualityInits/30_HospitalHCAHPS.asp

Deaton, C. (2001). Outcomes measurement and evidence-based nursing practice. *Journal of Cardiovascular Nursing, 15*(2), 83–86.

Deming, W. E. (2000). *Out of the crisis*. Cambridge, MA: MIT Press.

Donabedian, A. (1980). *The definition of quality and approaches to its assessment*. Ann Arbor, MI: Health Administration Press.

Dunham, R. B., & Pierce, J. L. (1989). *Management*. Glenview, IL: Scott Foresman and Company.

Epstein, R. M., & Street, R. L. (2007). *Patient-centered communication in cancer care: Promoting healing and reducing suffering*. Bethesda, MD: National Cancer Institute.

Evans, J. R., & Dean, J. W. (2003). *Total quality: Management, organization and strategy* (3rd ed.). Mason, OH: Thomson South-Western.

Every, N. R., Hochman, J., Becker, R., Kopecky, S., & Cannon, C. P., for the Committee on Acute Cardiac Care, Council on Clinical Cardiology, American Heart Association. (2000). Critical pathways: A review. *Circulation, 101,* 461–465. Retrieved from http://circ.ahajournals.org/content/101/4/461.full

Fisher, S., & Samways, M. (1985). *Write better behavioral objectives* (Infoline #5). Alexandria, VA: American Society for Training and Development.

Garvin, D. A. (1993). Building a learning organization. *Harvard Business Review, 71,* 78–91. Retrieved from http://w3.ualg.pt/~mzacaria/gic/HBR-Building-a-Leaning-Organization.pdf .

Gaucher, E. J., & Coffey, R. J. (1993). *Total quality in healthcare: From theory to practice.* San Francisco, CA: Jossey-Bass.

George, J. M. (1995). Leader positive mood and group performance: The case of customer service. *Journal of Applied Social Psychology, 25,* 778–794. doi:10.1111/j.1559-1816.1995.tb01775.x

George, J. M., & Jones, G. R. (2002). *Organizational behavior* (3rd ed.). Upper Saddle River, NJ: Prentice Hall.

Ginter, P. M., Swayne, L. E., & Duncan, W. J. (2002). *Strategic management of health care organizations* (4th ed.). Oxford, UK: Blackwell.

Glascow, R. (2002). *Technology and chronic care.* Paper presented at the Congress on Improving Chronic Care: Innovations in Research and Practice. September 8–10, Seattle, WA.

Greenberg, J., & Baron, R. A. (2003). *Behavior in organizations* (8th ed.). Upper Saddle River, NJ: Prentice Hall.

Greenhalgh, T. (1999). Narrative-based medicine in an evidence-based world. *British Medical Journal, 318,* 323–325. doi:10.1136/bmj.318.7179.323

Griffin, F. A., & Resar, R. K. (2009). *IHI Global Trigger Tool for measuring adverse events* (2nd ed.). IHI Innovation Series white paper. Cambridge, MA: Institute for Healthcare Improvement.

Hackman, J. R. (1987). The design of work teams. In J. W. Lorsch (Ed.), *Handbook of organizational behavior* (pp. 315–342). Upper Saddle River, NJ: Prentice Hall.

Herzberg, F., Maysner, B., & Snyderman, B. (1966). *Works and the nature of man.* New York, NY: John Wiley & Sons.

House, C., & Price, R. (1991). The return map: Track product teams. *Harvard Business Review, 60*(1), 93.

Hutchins, D. (2008). *Hoshin kanri: The strategic approach to continuous improvement.* Surrey, United Kingdom: Gower.

Institute for Healthcare Improvement. (n.d.). *Improvement advisor professional development program.* Retrieved from www.ihi.org/offerings/Training/ImprovementAdvisor/Pages/default.aspx

Institute of Medicine, Committee on Quality of Health Care in America. (2001). *Crossing the quality chasm: A new health system for the 21st century.* Washington, DC: National Academies Press.

Joint Commission on Accreditation of Healthcare Organizations (JCAHO). (1994). *Framework for improving performance: A guide for nurses.* Oakbrook Terrace, IL: Author.

Juran, J. M. (1989). *Juran on leadership for quality: An executive handbook.* New York, NY: The Free Press.

Kaplan, R., & Bower, M. (2001, March 15). The balanced scorecard and quality programs. *Balanced Scorecard Report* [Newsletter], pp. 3–6. Cambridge, MA: Harvard Business School Publishing.

Kaplan, R., & Norton, D. (1996). Using the balanced scorecard as a strategic management system. *Harvard Business Review, 74,* 75–85.

Kaplan, S., Greenfield, S., & Ware, J. E. (1989). Assessing the effects of physician-patient interactions on the outcomes of chronic disease. *Medical Care, 27*(3, supplement), S110–S127. doi:10.1097/00005650-198903001-00010

Katzenbach, J. R., & Smith, D. K. (1994). *The wisdom of teams: Creating the high-performance organization.* Boston, MA: Harvard Business School Press.

Kavaler, F., & Spiegel, A. (1997). *Risk management in health care institutions: A strategic approach.* Sudbury, MA: Jones & Bartlett.

Kelly, D. (2003). *Applying quality management in healthcare: A process for improvement.* Chicago, IL: Health Administration Press.

Kirkpatrick, D. L. (1998). *Evaluating training programs* (2nd ed.). San Francisco, CA: Berrett-Koehler.

Kline, P., & Saunders, B. (1998). *Ten steps to a learning organization* (2nd ed.). Arlington, VA: Great Ocean Publishers.

Kotter, J. P. (1990). What leaders really do. *Harvard Business Review, 68*, 103–111.

Kouzes, J. M., & Posner, B. Z. (2002). *Leadership: The challenge*. San Francisco, CA: Jossey-Bass.

Kuhn, A. M., & Youngberg, B. J. (2002). The need for risk management to evolve to assure a culture of safety. *Quality and Safety in Health Care, 11*, 158–162. doi:10.1136/qhc.11.2.158

Leatherman, S., Berwick, D., Illes, D., Lewin, L., Davidoff, F., Nolan, T., & Bisognano, M. (2003). The business case for quality: Case studies and an analysis. *Health Affairs, 22*(2), 17–30. doi:10.1377/hlthaff.22.2.17

Luecke, R. (2004). *Creating teams with an edge: The complete skill set to build powerful and influential teams*. Harvard Business Essentials Series. Boston, MA: Harvard Business School Press.

Luthans, F., Hodgetts, R., & Thompson, K. (1990). *Social issues in business: Strategic and public policy perspectives* (6th ed.). Upper Saddle River, NJ: Prentice Hall.

Maslow, A. (1954). *Motivation and personality*. New York, NY: Harper and Row.

McClelland, D. C., Atkinson, J. W., Clark, R. A., & Lowell, E. L. (1976). *The achievement motive*. New York, NY: Irvington.

National Partnership for Women and Families. (2012). Quality tool box: Consumer engagement. Retrieved from www.nationalpartnership.org/site/PageServer?pagename=qcn_ToolBox_ConsumerEngagement

National Quality Forum. (2011). *Guidance for evaluating the evidence related to the focus of quality measurement and importance to measure and report*. Washington, DC: Author.

Patient-Centered Outcomes Research Institute. (2012). Overview. Retrieved from www.pcori.org

Peters, T., & Waterman, R. (1982). *In search of excellence*. New York, NY: Harper & Row.

Phillips, J. (1996). How much is the training worth? *Training and Development, 50*(4), 20–24.

Phillips, J. J., & Phillips, P. P. (2003). *Manager's role in learning and performance*. Retrieved from http://media.roiinstitute.net/tools/2007/05/24/ManagersRoleinLeaningandPerformance.pdf

Phillips, J. J., & Phillips, P. P. (2005). *ROI at work: Best practice case studies from the real world*. Alexandria, VA: American Society for Training and Development.

Phillips, J., & Stone, R. (2002). *How to measure training results: A practical guide to tracking the six key indicators*. New York, NY: McGraw-Hill.

Provost, L., Miller, D., & Reinertsen, J. (2006). *A framework for leadership for improvement*. Cambridge, MA: Institute for Healthcare Improvement.

Robbins, S. P. (2001). *Organizational behavior* (8th ed.). Upper Saddle River, NJ: Prentice Hall.

Rogers, A. E., Hwang, W. T., Scott, L. D., Aiken, L. H., & Diages, D. F. (2004). The working hours of hospital staff nurses and patient safety. *Health Affairs, 23*(4), 202–212. doi:10.1377/hlthaff.23.4.202

Rokeach, M. (1973). *The nature of human values*. New York, NY: Free Press.

Rosati, R. J. (2003). Creating quality improvement projects. In E. L. Siegler, S. Mirafzali, & J. B. Foust (Eds.), *A guide to hospitals and inpatient care* (pp. 326–338). New York, NY: Springer.

Rotter, T., Kinsman, L., James, E. L., Machotta, A., Gothe, H., Willis, J., . . . Kugler, J. (2010). Clinical pathways: Effects on professional practice, patient outcomes, length of stay and hospital costs. *Cochrane Database of Systematic Reviews, 17*(3), CD006632. doi:10.1002/14651858.CD006632

Sackett, D., Rosenberg, W. M. C., Muir-Gray, J. A., Haynes, R. B., & Richardson, W. S. (1996). Evidence-based medicine: What it is and what it isn't. *British Medical Journal, 312*(13), 71–72. doi:10.1136/bmj.312.7023.71

Saunier, A. M., & Hawk, E. J. (1994). Realizing the potential of teams through team-based rewards. *Compensation & Benefits Review, 10*, 24–33. doi:10.1177/088636879402600404

Sawaya, G. F., Guirguis-Blake, J., LeFevre, M., Harris, R., Petitti, D., & U.S. Preventative Services Task Force. (2007). Update on the Methods: Estimating certainty and magnitude of net benefit. *Annals of Internal Medicine, 147*(12), 871–875.

Schein, E. H. (1992). *Organizational culture and leadership: A dynamic view* (2nd ed.). San Francisco, CA: Jossey-Bass.

Schneider, B. (Ed.). (1990). *Organizational culture and climate.* San Francisco, CA: Jossey-Bass.

Scholtes, P. R., Joiner, B. L., & Streibel, B. (2003). *The team handbook* (3rd ed.). Madison, WI: Joiner/Oriel.

Schwarz, M., Landis, S., & Rowe, J. (1999, April). A team approach to quality improvement. *Family Practice Management, 6,* 25–31.

Senge, P. M. (1990). *The fifth discipline: The art & practice of the learning organization.* New York, NY: Doubleday.

Sharp HealthCare. (2012). The Sharp Experience. Retrieved from www.sharp.com/choose-sharp/sharp-experience

Shortell, S. M., Morrison, E., & Robbins, S. (1985). Strategy-making in health care organizations: A framework and agenda for research. *Medical Care Review, 2,* 219–266. doi:10.1177/107755878504200203

Siehl, L., & Martin, J. (1981). *Learning organizational culture* [Working paper]. Palo Alto, CA: Stanford University Graduate School of Business.

SSM Health Care. (n.d.). SSM Health Care home page. Retrieved from www.ssmhc.com/internet/home/ssmcorp.nsf

StoryCorps. (2012). About us. Retrieved from http://storycorps.org/about

Studer Group. (2012). *The five pillars.* Retrieved from www.studergroup.com/dotCMS/knowledgeAssetDetail?inode=109970

Thompson, L. (2000). *Making the team: A guide for managers.* Upper Saddle River, NJ: Prentice Hall.

Tonelli, M. (2001). The limits of evidence-based medicine. *Respiratory Care, 46*(12), 1435–1440. doi:10.1097/00001888-199812000-00011

Tuckman, W. (1965). Developmental sequence in small groups. *Psychological Bulletin, 63,* 384–399. doi:10.1037/h0022100

U.S. Department of Energy, Office of Management. (n.d.). Balanced scorecard program. Retrieved from http://energy.gov/management/office-management/operational-management/procurement-and-acquisition/balanced-scorecard

U.S. Department of Health and Human Services. (2011). Partnership for Patients: A common commitment. Retrieved from www.healthcare.gov/compare/partnership-for-patients/about/index.html

U.S. Preventative Services Task Force. (2008). Grade definitions. Retrieved from www.uspreventiveservicestaskforce.org/uspstf/grades.htm

Von Korff, M., Gruman, J., Schaeffer, J., Curry, S. J., & Wagner, E. H. (1997). Collaborative management of chronic illness. *Annals of Internal Medicine, 127*(12), 1097–1102.

Wageman, R. (1997). Critical success factors for creating superb self-managing teams. *Organizational Dynamics, 26,* 49–61. doi:10.1016/S0090-2616(97)90027-9

White, S. V. (2004). Interview with a quality leader: David Brailer on information technology and advancing healthcare quality. *Journal for Healthcare Quality, 26*(6), 20–25. doi:10.1111/j.1945-1474.2004.tb00531.x

Zander, K., & Bower, K. (1987). *Nursing case management, blueprint for transformation.* Boston, MA: New England Medical Center Hospitals.

Zuzelo, P. R. (2010). *The clinical nurse specialist handbook* (2nd. ed). Sudbury, MA: Jones and Bartlett.

Suggested Reading

Abi Rafeh, N., Abi-Fadel, D., Wetz, R. Y., Khoueiry, G., Azab, B., Edwards, A., ... Costantino, T. (2009). A STEMI code protocol improves door-to-balloon time on weekdays and weekends. *Journal of Healthcare Quality, 31*(6), 35–43. doi:10.1111/j.1945-1474.2009.00053.x

Al-Araidah, O., Momani, A., Khasawneh, M., & Momani, M. (2010). Lead-time reduction utilizing lean tools applied to healthcare: The inpatient pharmacy at a local hospital. *Journal for Healthcare Quality, 32*(1), 59–66. doi:10.1111/j.1945-1474.2009.00065.x

Alrashdan, A., Momani, A., & Ababneh, T. (2012). Activities identification for activity-based cost/management applications of the diagnostics outpatient procedures. *Journal for Healthcare Quality, 34*(1), 35–43. doi:10.1111j.1945-1474.2011.00139.x

American Association of Critical Care Nurses. (2012). *Beacon Award for Excellence™*. Retrieved from www.aacn.org/wd/beaconapps/content/mainpage.pcms?menu=beaconapps

American Nurses Credentialing Center. (2012). *Magnet Recognition Program®*. Retrieved from www.nursecredentialing.org/Magnet.aspx

Anderson, B. L., Strunk, A. L. & Schulkin, J. (2011). Study on defensive medicine practices among obstetricians and gynecologists who provide breast care. *Journal for Healthcare Quality, 33*(3), 37–43. doi:10.111/j.1945-1474.2010.00120.x

Anderson, R. A., & McDaniel, R. R. (2000). Managing health care organizations: Where professionalism meets complex science. *Health Care Management Review, 25*(1), 83–92. doi:10.1097/00004010-200001000-00010

Annbruster, R. R., Begun, 1. W. & Duncan, A. K. (2009). An in-house learning laboratory for patient-centered innovation. *Journal for Healthcare Quality, 31*(1), 10–17. doi:10.1111/j.1945-1474.2009.00004.x

Asadoorian, J., Hearson, B., Satyanarayana, S., & Ursel, J. (2010). Evidence-based practice in healthcare: an exploratory cross-discipline comparison of enhancers and barriers. *Journal for Healthcare Quality, 32*(3), 15–22. doi:10.1111/j.1945-1474.2010.00081.x

Atkinson, J. G., Masiulis, K. E., Feigner, L. & Schumacher, D. N. (2010). Provider-Initiated Pay-for-Performance in a Clinically Integrated Hospital Network. *Journal for Healthcare Quality, 32*(1), 42–50. doi:10.1111j.1945-1474.2009.00063.x

Bailit, M., & Dyer, M. (2004). *Beyond bankable dollars: Establishing a business case for improving healthcare*. New York, NY: The Commonwealth Fund.

Baldrige Performance Excellence Program. (2011–2012). *Health care criteria for performance excellence*. Retrieved from www.nist.gov/baldrige/publications/hc_criteria.cfm

Barry, T. L., Kaiser, K. L., Lopez, P. & McNulty, M. E. (2009). Participant satisfaction methods and outcomes in Medicaid managed care. *Journal for Healthcare Quality, 31*(1), 21–29. doi:10.1111/j.1945.1474.2009.000022.x

Barry, R., Murcko, A. C., & Brubaker, C. E. (2002). *The Six Sigma book for healthcare*. Chicago, IL: Health Administration Press.

Batalden, P. B., & Buchanan, E. D. (1989). Industrial models of quality improvement. In N. Goldfield & D. Nash (Eds.), *Providing quality care* (pp. 133–159). Philadelphia, PA: American College of Physicians.

Bates, D. W., & Gawande, A. A. (2003). Improving safety with information technology. *New England Journal of Medicine, 348*, 2526–2534. doi:10.1056/NEJMsa020847

Bauer, M., Fitzgerald, L. & Koch, S. (20 11). Hospital discharge as experienced by family carers of people with dementia: a case for quality improvement. *Journal for Healthcare Quality, 33*(6), 9–16. doi:10.1111/j.1945-1474.2011.00122..x

Becher, E. C., & Chassin, M. R. (2001). Improving the quality of healthcare: Who will lead? *Health Affairs, 20*, 164–179. doi:10.1377/hlthaff.20.5.164

Beckett, C. D. & Kipnis, G. (2009). Collaborative communication: integrating SBAR to improve quality/patient safety outcomes. *Journal for Healthcare Quality, 31*(5), 19–28. doi:10.1111/j.1945-1474.2009.00043.x

Berwick, D. M. (1989). Continuous improvement as an ideal in health care. *New England Journal of Medicine, 320*, 53–56. doi:10.1056/NEJM198901053200110

Berwick, D. M., Godfrey, A. B., & Roessner, J. (1990). *Curing health care*. San Francisco, CA: Jossey-Bass.

Binhas, M., Roudot -Thoraval , F., Bonnet, F., Guerineau, S., Lory, C., Jeanblanc, G., ... Marty, J. (2011). Use of a validated reference tool to evaluate postoperative pain management through a quality-improvement program in a university hospital. *Journal for Healthcare Quality, 33*(1), 7–13. doi:10.1111/j.1945-1474.2010.00096.x

Black, J. (2009). Transforming the patient care environment with lean six sigma and realistic evaluation. *Journal for Healthcare Quality, 31*(3), 29–35. doi:10.1111/j.1945-1474.2009.00028.x

Brown, D. S., Donaldson, N., Burnes Bolton, L., & Aydin, C. E. (2010). Nursing sensitive benchmarks for hospitals to gauge high-reliability performance. *Journal for Healthcare Quality, 32*(6), 9–17. doi:10.1111/j.1945-1474.2010.00083.x

Burke, D., Menachemi, N., & Brooks, R. G. (2005). Diffusion of information technology supporting the Institute of Medicine's quality chasm care aims. *Journal for Healthcare Quality, 27*(1), 24–32. doi:10.1111/j.1945-1474.2005.tb00542.x

Byers, J. F., & Aragon, E. D. (2003). What quality improvement professionals need to know about IRBs. *Journal for Healthcare Quality, 25*(4), 4–9. doi:10.1111/j.1945-1474.2003.tb01067.x

Byers, J. F., & White, S. V. (Eds.). (2004). *Patient safety: Principles and practice* (pp. 87–134). New York, NY: Springer.

Calhoun, B. C., Goode, J. & Simmons, K. (2011). Process improvement of pap smear tracking in a women's medicine center clinic in residency training. *Journal for Healthcare Quality, 33*(6), 25–32. doi:10.1111/j.1945-1474.2011.00129.x

Chang, Y. J., Siegel, B. & Wilkerson, G. (2012). Measuring healthcare disparities and racial segregation in Missouri nursing homes. *Journal for Healthcare Quality, 34*(1), 16–25. doi:10.1111/j.1945-1474.2011.00135.x

Chassin, M. R. (1998). Is health care ready for six sigma quality? *The Milbank Quarterly, 76*(4), 565–591. Retrieved from www.milbank.org/quarterly/764featchas.html

Chen, J. Y., Kang, N., Juarez, D. T., Hodges, K. A. & Chung, R. S. (2010). Impact of a Pay-for-Performance Program on Low Performing Physicians. *Journal for Healthcare Quality, 32*(1), 13–22. doi:10.1111/j.1945-1474.2009.00059.x

Chen, J. Y., Kang, N., Juarez, D. T., Yennilov, I., Braithwaite, R. S., Hodges, K. A.,...Chung, R. S. (201 1). Heart failure patients receiving ACEIs/ARBs were less likely to be hospitalized or to use emergency care in the following year. *Journal for Healthcare Quality, 33*(4), 29–36. doi:10.1111/j.1945-1474.2010.00124.x

Codman, E. A. (1916 & 1972). *A study of hospital efficiency*. Ann Arbor, MI: University Microfilms.

Coffman, J. M., Sergo, J. A., & Spetz, J. (2002). Minimum nurse-to-patient ratios in acute care hospitals in California. *Health Affairs, 21*(Suppl.), 53–64. doi:10.1377/hlthaff.21.5.53

Comans, T. A., Clark, M. J., Cartmill, L., Ash, S. & Sheppard, L. A. (2011). How do allied health professionals evaluate new models of care? What are we measuring and why? *Journal for Healthcare Quality, 33*(4), 19–28. doi:10.1111/j1945-1474.2011.00152.x

Covey, S. R. (1989). *The seven habits of highly effective people.* New York, NY: Simon & Schuster.

Cramer, S., Chapa, G., Kotsos, T. & Jenich, H. (2010). Assessing multiple hospitalizations for health-plan-managed Medicaid diabetic members. *Journal for Healthcare Quality, 32*(3), 7–14. doi:10.1111/j.1945-1474.2010.000089.x

Crozier, C., Erickson-Wittmann, B., Movsas, B., Owen, J., Khalid, N., & Wilson, J. F. (2011). Shifting the focus to practice quality improvement in radiation oncology. *Journal for Healthcare Quality, 33*(5), 49–57. doi:10.1111 /j.1945-1474.2011.00119.x

Daniel, L. T. & Simpson, E. K. (2009). Integrating team training strategies into obstetrical emergency simulation training. *Journal for Healthcare Quality, 31*(5), 38–42. doi:10.1111/j.1945-1474.2009.00045.x

Deming, W. E. (2000). *The new economics for industry, government, education.* Cambridge, MA: MIT Press.

DeWolf, L. (2009). Understanding Innovation in Healthcare. *Journal for Healthcare Quality, 31*(1), 3–4. doi:10.1111/j.1945-1474.2009.00001.x

Dhar, S., Michel, R. & Kanna, B. (2011). Improving visit cycle time using patient flow analysis in a high-volume inner-city hospital-based ambulatory clinic serving minority New Yorkers. *Journal for Healthcare Quality, 33*(2), 23–28. doi:10.1111/j.1945-1474.2010.00111.x

Donabedian, A. (1980). *Exploration in quality assessment and monitoring*. Ann Arbor, MI: Health Administration Press.

Dowling, D. A. (2010). Interview with a Quality Leader: Michael Bailit on Pay-for-Performance. *Journal for Healthcare Quality, 32*(1), 10–12. doi:10.1111/j.1945-1474.2009.00058.x

Elgart, L. & Gaffney, A. (2009). Advancing patient safety through process improvements. *Journal for Healthcare Quality, 31*(5), 8–13. doi:10.1111/j.1945-1474.2009.00041.x

Eller, A. (2009). Rapid assessment and disposition: Applying LEAN in the emergency department. *Journal for Healthcare Quality, 31*(3), 17–22. doi:10.1111/j.1945-1474.2009.00026.x

Etzel-Hardman, D., Kapsin, K., Jones, S., & Churilla, H. (2009). Sedation reduction in a pediatric radiology department. *Journal for Healthcare Quality, 31*(4), 34–39. doi:10.1111/j.1945-1474.2009.00035.x

Flores, D. M. (2009). Q&A: Annette Tonen on a geriatrics framework for home care: A quality improvement approach. *Journal for Healthcare Quality, 31*(2), 54–56. doi:10.1111/j.1945-1474.2009.00019.x

Fogg, J. T. (2010). Interview with a quality leader: Dale W. Bratzler, DO, MPH on performance measures. *Journal for Healthcare Quality, 32*(2), 24–28. doi:10.1111/j.1945-174.2009.00077.x

Fottler, M. D., Ford, R. C., & Heaton, C. P. (2002). *Achieving service excellence: Strategies for healthcare*. Chicago, IL: Health Administration Press.

Fried, B. J., & Johnson, J. A. (2001). *Human resources in healthcare: Managing for success*. Chicago, IL: Health Administration Press.

Garcia-Caban, L A. (2010). Pay-for-Performance: Quality Programs at the Crossroads. *Journal for Healthcare Quality, 32*(1), 3–7. doi:10.1111/j.1945-1474.2009.00056.x

Gaucher, E. J., & Coffey, R. J. (2000). *Breakthrough performance: Accelerating the transformation of health care organizations*. San Francisco, CA: Jossey-Bass.

Gaucher, E. M., & Coffey, R. J. (1991). *Transforming healthcare organizations: How to achieve and sustain organizational excellence*. San Francisco, CA: Jossey-Bass.

Graham, J. M., Brinson, M., Magtibay, L.-Y., Regan, B., & Lazar, E. J. (2009). Virtual patient safety rounds: One hospital system's approach to sharing knowledge. *Journal for Healthcare Quality, 31*(5), 48–52. doi:10.111/j.1945-1474.2009.00047.x

Griffith, J. R., & White, K. R. (2003). *Thinking forward: Six strategies for highly successful organizations*. Chicago, IL: Health Administration Press.

Hadelman, J. (2000). *The impact of strategic healthcare leadership: Top ten leadership trends in health care in the 21st century*. Oak Brook, IL: Witt/Kieffer.

Hansen, J. P. (2003). CAN'T MISS: Conquer any number task by making important statistics simple. Part 1. Types of variables, mean, median, variance, and standard deviation. *Journal for Healthcare Quality, 25*(4), 19–24. doi:10.1111/j.1945-1474.2003.tb01070.x

Hansen, J. P. (2003). CAN'T MISS: Conquer any number task by making important statistics simple. Part 2. Probability, populations, samples, and normal distributions. *Journal for Healthcare Quality, 25*(4), 25–33. doi:10.1111/j.1945-1474.2003.tb01071.x

Hansen, J. P. (2003). CAN'T MISS: Conquer any number task by making important statistics simple. Part 3. Standard error, estimation, and confidence intervals. *Journal for Healthcare Quality, 25*(4), 34–39. doi:10.1111/j.1945-1474.2003.tb01072.x

Hansen, J. P. (2004). CAN'T MISS: Conquer any number task by making important statistics simple. Part 4. Confidence intervals with *t* distributions, standard error, and confidence intervals for proportions. *Journal for Healthcare Quality, 26*(4), 26–32. doi:10.1111/j.1945-1474.2004.tb00504.x

Hansen, J. P. (2004). CAN'T MISS: Conquer any number task by making important statistics simple. Part 5. Comparing two confidence intervals, standard error of the difference between two means and between two proportions. *Journal for Healthcare Quality, 26*(4), 33–42. doi:10.1111/j.1945-1474.2004.tb00506.x

Hansen, J. P. (2004). CAN'T MISS: Conquer any number task by making important statistics simple. Part 6. Tests of statistical significance (z test statistic, rejecting the null hypothesis, p value), t test, z test for proportions, statistical significance versus meaningful difference. *Journal for Healthcare Quality, 26*(4), 43–53. doi:10.1111/j.1945-1474.2004.tb00507.x

Hansen, J. P. (2005). CAN'T MISS: Conquer any number task by making important statistics simple. Part 7. Statistical process control: *x–s* control charts. *Journal for Healthcare Quality, 27*(4), 32–43. doi:10.1111/j.1945-1474.2005.tb00566.x

Hansen, J. P. (2005). CAN'T MISS: Conquer any number task by making important statistics simple. Part 8. Statistical process control: *n, np, c, u* control charts. *Journal for Healthcare Quality, 27*(4), 45–52. doi:10.1111/j.1945-1474.2005.tb00567.x

Harlan, G. A, Nkoy, F. L., Srivastava, R., Lattin, G., Wolfe, D., Mundorff, M. B.,...Maloney, C. G. (2010). Improving Transitions of care at hospital discharge implications for pediatric hospitalists and primary care providers. *Journal for Healthcare Quality, 32*(5), 51–60. doi:10.1111/j.1945-1474.2010.00105.x

Harry, M., & Schroeder, R. (2000). *Six sigma: The breakthrough strategy revolutionizing the world's top corporations.* New York, NY: Currency/Doubleday.

Hatlem, T., Jones, C., & Woodard, E. K. (2011). Reducing mortality and avoiding preventable ICU utilization: Analysis of a successful rapid response program using APRDRGs. *Journal for Healthcare Quality, 33*(5), 7–16. doi:10.1111/j.1945-1474.2011.00084.x

Helmrich, R. L., & Merritt, A. C. (1998). *Culture at work in aviation and medicine.* Aldershot, England: Ashgate.

Hess, R. G. (2004). From bedside to boardroom: Nursing shared governance. *Online Journal of Issues in Nursing, 9*(1), 3. Retrieved from www.nursingworld.org/ojin/topic23/tpc23_1.htm

Horak, B. J. (1997). *Strategic planning in healthcare: Building a quality-based plan step-by-step.* Portland, OR: Book News.

Huggins, E. J. (2010). Lean methodology: Supporting battlefield medical fitness by cutting process waste. *Journal for Healthcare Quality, 32*(4), 39–49. doi:10.1111/j.1945-1474.201 0.00087.x

Hunt, S., Henry, L. & Ad, N. (2011). Using Multiple Databases to Produce Comprehensive Follow-Up in an Effort to Enhance Evaluation of Outcome Measurements: Surgical Ablation (Maze) Exemplar. *Journal for Healthcare Quality, 33*(3), 50–63. doi:10.1111/j.1945-1474.2010.00126.x

Institute of Medicine, Committee on Quality of Health Care in America. (2000). *To err is human: Building a safer health system.* Washington, DC: National Academies Press.

Integrated Healthcare Association. (2005). *California leadership group of health plans, physician groups, and health systems.* Retrieved from www.iha.org

James, B. C. (1990). *Quality management for health care delivery.* Chicago, IL: The Hospital Research and Education Trust.

Jha, A. K., Stone, R., Lave, J., Chen, H., Klusaritz, H., & Volpp, K. (2010). The concentration of hospital care for Black veterans in Veterans Affairs hospitals: Implications for clinical outcomes. *Journal for Healthcare Quality, 32*(6), 52–61. doi:10.1111/j.1945-1474.2010.00085.x

Jin, L. X., Ibrahim, A. M., Newman, N. A., Makarov, D. V., Pronovost, P. J., & Makary, M. A. (2011). Robotic surgery claims on United States hospital websites. *Journal for Healthcare Quality, 33*(6), 48–52. doi:10.1111/j.1945-1474.2011.00148.x

The Joint Commission. (n.d.). *Alternatives for sharing sentinel event related information with The Joint Commission.* Retrieved from www.jointcommission.org/se_alternatives

Jones, D., & Womack, J. (2003). *Lean thinking: Banish waste and create wealth in your corporation* (Rev. ed.). New York, NY: Free Press.

Jones, M., Hsu, C., Pearson, D., Wolford, D. & Labby, D. (2011). An Alternative to Pay-for-Performance: One Health Plan's Approach to Quality Improvement. *Journal for Healthcare Quality, 33*(1), 22–29. doi:10.1111/j.1945-1474.2010.00100.x

Juran, J. M. (1967, January). The QC circle phenomenon. *Industrial Control, 23,* 329–336.

Juran, J. M. (1977). *Quality and its assurance: An overview.* Presented at the Second NATO Symposium on Quality and Its Assurance, London, England.

Juran, J. M. (1981, June). Product quality: A prescription for the west. *The Management Review.* (Presented at the 25th Conference of the European Organization for Quality Control, Paris, France).

Kibler, J., & Lee, M. (2011). Improving patient transfer between the intensive care unit and the Medical/surgical floor of a 200-bed hospital in southern California. *Journal for Healthcare Quality, 33*(1), 68– 76. doi:10.1111/j.1945-1474.2010.00101.x

Knapp, H., Fletcher, M., Taylor, A., Chan, K., & Goetz, M. B. (2011). No clinic left behind: Providing cost-effective in-services via distance learning. *Journal for Healthcare Quality, 33*(5), 17–24. doi:10.111/j.1945-1474.2010.00117.x

Kolbasovsky, A., & Reich, L. (2010). Improving the quality of diabetes care: A behavioral health intervention. *Journal for Healthcare Quality, 32*(2), 43–51. doi:10.1111/j.1945-1474.2009.00067.x

Kotter, J. P. (1995, March–April). Why transformation efforts fail. *Harvard Business Review*, 59–67.

Kotter, J. P. (1996). *Leading change*. Boston, MA: Harvard Business School Press.

LaRocco, M., & Brient, K. (2010). Interdisciplinary process improvement for enhancing blood transfusion safety. *Journal for Healthcare Quality, 32*, 29–34. doi:10.1111/j.1945-1474.2009.00070.x

Magill, M. K., Day, J., Mervis, A., Donnelly, S. M., Parsons, M., Baker, ... Bun, R. (2009). Improving colonoscopy referral rates through computer-supported, primary care practice redesign. *Journal for Healthcare Quality, 31*(4), 43–53. doi:10.1111/j.1945-1474.2009.00037.x

Martin, K. (2003). On lean enterprise and its potential healthcare applications [Editorial]. *Journal for Healthcare Quality, 25*(5), 2, 43. doi:10.1111/j.1945-1474.2003.tb01080.x

McCue, J. D., Beck, A., & Smothers, K. (2009). Quality toolbox: Clinical pathways can improve core measure scores. *Journal for Healthcare Quality, 31*(1), 43–50. doi:10.1111/j.1945-1474.2009.00008.x

McLaughlin, C. P., & Kaluzny, A. D. (1999). *Continuous quality improvement in health care: Theory, implementation, and applications* (2nd ed.). Gaithersburg, MD: Aspen.

Menachemi, N., Powers, T., Au, D. W. & Brooks, R. G. (2010). Predictors of Physician Satisfaction among Electronic Health Record System Users. *Journal for Healthcare Quality, 32*(1), 35–41. doi:10.1111/j.1945-1474.2009.00062.x

Morse, R. B., & Pollack, M. M. (2012). Root cause analyses performed in a children's hospital: Events, action plan strength, and implementation rates. *Journal for Healthcare Quality, 34*(1), 55–61. doi:10.1111/j.1945-1474.2011.00140.x

Nash, M., Pestrue, J., Geier, P., Sharp, K., Helder, A., & McAlearney, A. S. (20 10). Leveraging information technology to drive improvement in patient satisfaction. *Journal for Healthcare Quality, 32*(5), 30–40. doi:10.1111/j.1945-1474.2010.00110.x

National Association for Healthcare Quality (NAHQ). (2011). *NAHQ code of ethics and standards of practice for healthcare quality professionals*. Glenview, IL: Author. Retrieved from www.nahq.org/Quality-Community/content/codeethicspractice.html

National Committee for Quality Assurance. (2011). *HEDIS 2011* (Vols. 1 & 2). Washington, DC: Author.

National Quality Forum. (2011). *Serious reportable events in healthcare—2011 update: A consensus report*. Washington, DC: Author.

Newell, T. L., Steinmetz-Malato, L. L. & Van Dyke, D. L. (2011). Applying Toyota Production System Techniques for Medication Delivery: Improving Hospital Safety and Efficiency. *Journal for Healthcare Quality, 33*(2), 15–22. doi:10.1111/j.1945-1474.2010.00104.x

Nowalk, M. P., Lin, C. 1., Zimmerman, R. K., Fox, D. E., Raymund, M., Tanis, M. D., & Harper, J. D. (2010). Establish the habit: Influenza vaccination for health care personnel. *Journal for Healthcare Quality, 32*(2), 35–42. doi:10.1111/j.1945-1474.2010.00073.x

Oh, H. C., Toh, H. G. & Giap Cheong, E. S. (2011). Realization of process improvement at a diagnostic radiology department with aid of simulation modeling. *Journal for Healthcare Quality, 33*(6), 40–47. doi:10.1111/j.1945-1474.2011.00133.x

Osborne, M., Graham, J., Cowley, K., Hundley, D. D., & Chambers, D. (2010). Because one is too many: Catholic Health Initiatives' success in reducing preventable birth injuries. *Journal for Healthcare Quality, 32*, 24–30. doi:10.1111/j.1945-1474.2010.00080.x

Pelletier, L. R. (2000). On error-free healthcare: Mission possible! [Editorial]. *Journal for Healthcare Quality, 22*(3), 2. doi:10.1111/j.1945-1474.2000.tb00118.x

Peterman, J. M., & Bisgaard, S. (2010). Door-to-balloon time: Performance improvement in the multidisciplinary treatment of myocardial infarction. *Journal for Healthcare Quality, 32*(4), 14–23. doi:10.1111/j.1945-1474.2010.00079.x

Peterson, G. M., Thompson, A., Pulver, L K., Robertson, M. B., Brieger, D., Wai, A., & Ten, S. E. for the DMACS Project Group. (2012). Management of acute coronary syndromes at hospital discharge: Do targeted educational interventions improve practice quality? *Journal for Healthcare Quality, 34*(1), 26–34. doi:10.1111/j.1945-1474.2011.00137.x

Pham, J. C , Andrawis, M., Shore, A. D., Fahey, M., Morlock, L., & Pronovost, P. J. (2011). Are temporary staff associated with more severe emergency department medication errors? *Journal for Healthcare Quality, 33*(4), 9–18. doi:10.1111/j.1945-1474.2010.00116.x

Plsek, P., & Omnias, A. (1989). *Juran Institute quality improvement tools: Problem solving/glossary*. Wilton, CT: Juran Institute.

Pointer, D. D., & Ewell, C. M. (1995). Really governing: What type of work should boards be doing? *Journal of Healthcare Management, 40*(3), 315–332.

Porter-O'Grady, T., Hawkins, M. A., & Parker, M. L. (1997). *Whole-systems shared governance: Architecture for integration*. Gaithersburg, MD: Aspen.

Pracht, E. E., & Bass, E. (2011). Exploring the link between ambulatory care and avoidable hospitalizations at the Veteran Health Administration. *Journal for Healthcare Quality, 33*(2), 47–56. doi:10.1111/j.1945-1474.2010.00125.x

Pracht, E. E., Orban, B. L., Comins, M. M., Large, J. T. & Asin-Oostburg, V. (2011). The Relative Effectiveness of Managed Care Penetration and the Healthcare Safety Net in Reducing Avoidable Hospitalizations. *Journal for Healthcare Quality, 33*(4), 42–53. doi:10.1111/j.1945-1474.2011.00154.x

President's Information Technology Advisory Committee. (2004). *Health Care Delivery and Information Technology Subcommittee: Draft recommendations, April 13, 2004*. Retrieved from www.itrd.gov/pitac/.../2004/20040413/20040413_draft_hit.pdf

Rauch, K., Balascio, J., & Gilbert, P. (2009). Excellence in action: developing and implementing a fall prevention program. *Journal for Healthcare Quality, 31*(1), 36–42. doi:10. 1111/j. 1945-1474.2009.00007.x

Revere, L., & Black, K. (2003). Integrating Six Sigma with total quality management: A case example for measuring medication errors. *Journal of Healthcare Management, 48*(6), 377–391.

Rhodes, N., McVay, T., Harrington, L., Luquire, R., Winter, M., & Helms, B. (2009). Eliminating catheter-associated urinary tract infections: Part II. Limit duration of catheter use. *Journal for Healthcare Quality, 31*(6), 13– 17. doi:10.1111/j.1945-1474.2009.00050.x

Roberts, J. S., Redman, R. R., & Coate, J. G. (1987). A history of The Joint Commission on Accreditation of Hospitals. *JAMA, 258*, 936–940. doi:10.1001/jama.258.7.936

Roberts, K. H., & Bea, R. (2001). Must accidents happen? Lessons from high-reliability organizations. *Academy of Management Executive, 15*, 70–78. doi:10.5465/AME.2001.5229613

Rodriguez, M. A., Tortorella, F., & St. John, C. (2010). Improving psychosocial care for improved health outcomes. *Journal for Healthcare Quality, 32*(4), 3–13. doi:10.1111/j.1945-1474.2010.00099.x

Rosati, R. J., Marren, J. M., Davin, D. M., & Morgan, C. J. (2009). The linkage between employee and patient satisfaction in home healthcare. *Journal for Healthcare Quality, 31*(2), 44–53. doi:10.1111/j. 1945-1474.2009.00018.x

Russell, D., Rosati, R. J., Rosenfeld, P., & Marren, J. M. (2011). Continuity in home health care: Is consistency in nursing personnel associated with better patient outcomes? *Journal for Healthcare Quality, 33*(6), 33–39. doi:10.1111/j.1945-1474.2011.00131.x

Russell, D., Rosati, R. J., Sobolewski, S., Marten, J., & Rosenfeld, P. (2011). Implementing a transitional care program for high-risk heart failure patients: Findings from a community-based partnership between a certified home healthcare agency and regional hospital. *Journal for Healthcare Quality, 33*(6), 17–24. doi:10.1111/j.1945-1474.2011.00167.x

Russell, D., Rosenfeld, P., Ames, S., & Rosati, R. J. (2010). Using technology to enhance the quality of home health care: Three case studies of health information technology initiatives at the visiting nurse service of New York. *Journal for Healthcare Quality, 32*(5), 22–29. doi:10.1111/j. 1945-1474.2010.00098.x

Ryvicker, M., Feldman, P. H., Rosati, R. 1., Sobolewski, S., Maduro, G. A., & Schwartz, T. (2011). Improving functional outcomes in home care patients: Impact and challenges of disseminating a quality improvement initiative. *Journal for Healthcare Quality, 33*(5), 28–36. doi:10.1111/j.1945 -1474.2011.00156.x

Sanderson, B. K., Thompson, J., Brown, T M., Tucker, M. J., & Bittner, V. (2009). Assessing patient recall of discharge instructions for acute myocardial infarction. *Journal for Healthcare Quality, 31*(6), 25–34. doi:10.1111/j.1945-1474.2009.00052.x

Sedlack, J. D. (2010). The utilization of Six Sigma and statistical process control techniques in surgical quality improvement. *Journal for Healthcare Quality, 32*(6), 18–26. doi:10.1111/j.1945-1474.2010.00102.x

Shea-Lewis, A. (2009). Teamwork: Crew resource management in a community hospital. *Journal for Healthcare Quality, 31*(5), 14–18. doi:10.1111/j.1945-1474.2009.00042.x

Shively, M., Rutledge, T., Rose, B. A., Graham, P., Long, R., Stucky, E., ... Dresselhaus, T. (2011). Real-time assessment of nurse work environment and stress. *Journal for Healthcare Quality, 33*(1), 39–48. doi:10.1111/j.1945-1474.2010.00093.x

Shortell, S. M., & Kaluzny, A. D. (2005). *Health care management: Organization design and behavior*. Albany, NY: Delmar Thomson Learning.

Silich, S. J., WelZ. R. Y., RieblIng, N., Coleman, C., Khoueiry, G., Rafeh, N. A.,...Szerszen, A. (2012). Using Six Sigma methodology to reduce patient transfer times from floor to critical-care beds. *Journal for Healthcare Quality, 34*(1), 44–54. doi:10.1111/j.1945-1474.2011.00184.x

Smith, C., Wood, S., & Beauvais, B. (2011). Thinking Lean: Implementing DMAIC methods to improve efficiency within a cystic fibrosis clinic. *Journal for Healthcare Quality, 33*(2), 37–46. doi:10.1111 /j.1945-1474.2010.00130.x

Snyder, K. D., & McDermott, M. (2009). A rural hospital takes on Lean. *Journal for Healthcare Quality, 31*(3), 23–28. doi:10.1111/j.1945-1474.2009.00027.x

Soo Hoo, W. E., Muehlberg, K., Ferraro, R. G., & Jumaoas, M. C. (2009). Successes and lessons learned implementing the sepsis bundle. *Journal for Healthcare Quality, 31*(4), 9–15. doi:11.1111 /j.1945-1474.2009.00032.x

Sutton, G., Liao, J., Jimmieson, N. L., & Restubog, S. L. D. (2011). Measuring multidisciplinary team effectiveness in a ward-based healthcare setting: Development of the team functioning assessment tool. *Journal for Healthcare Quality, 33*(3), 10–24. doi:10.01111 /j.1945-1474.2011.00138.x

Tague, N. R. (2005). *The quality toolbox* (2nd ed.). Milwaukee, WI: American Society for Quality, Quality Press.

Thompson, A. A. Jr., & Strickland, A. J. III. (1996). *Strategic management: Concepts and cases* (9th ed.). Boston, MA: Irwin McGraw-Hill.

Travis, J., Carr, J. B., Saylor, D., King, A., Bence, W., Key, S.,...Trienski, T. (2009). Coronary artery bypass graft surgery: Surgical site infection prevention. *Journal for Healthcare Quality, 31*(4), 16–23. doi:10.1111/j.1945-1474.2009.00033.x

Tyler, J. L., & Biggs, E. (2001). *Practical governance*. Chicago, IL: Health Administration Press.

Vallejo, B. (2009). Tools of the trade: Lean and Six Sigma. *Journal for Healthcare Quality, 31*(3), 3–4. doi:10.1111/j.1945-1474.2009.00023.x

Van Kleek, E., Liu, S., Conn, L. M., Hoadley, A., & Ho, S. B. (2010). Improving the effectiveness of fecal occult blood testing in a primary care clinic by direct colonoscopy referral for positive tests. *Journal for Healthcare Quality, 32*(6), 62–69. doi:10.1111/j.1945-1474.2009.00071.x

Vinson, D. R. & Patel, P. B. (2009). Facilitating follow-up after emergency care using an appointment assignment system. *Journal for Healthcare Quality, 31*(6), 18–24. doi:10.1111/j.1945-14 74.2009.00051.x

Voinea-Griffin, A, Rindal, D. B., Fellows, J. L., Barasch, A., Gilbert, G. H., Safford, M. M., & for the DPBRN Collaborative Group. (2010). Pay-for-performance in dentistry: What we know. *Journal for Healthcare Quality, 32*(1), 51–58. doi:10.1111/j.1945-1474.2009.00064.x

Wagner, B., Meirowitz, N., Shah, J., Nanda, D., Reggio, L., Cohen, P.,et al. (2012). Comprehensive perinatal safety initiative to reduce adverse obstetric events. *Journal for Healthcare Quality, 34*(1), 6–15. doi:10.1111/j.1945-1474.2011.00134.x

Watkins, K. E., Horvitz-Lennon, M., Caldarone, L. 8., Shugannan, L. R., Smith, B., Mannle, T. E.,...Pincus, H. A (201 1). Developing medical record-based performance indicators to measure the quality of mental healthcare. *Journal for Healthcare Quality, 33*(1), 49–67. doi:10.1111/j.1945-1474.2010.00128.x

Watkins, K. E., Keyser, D. J., Smith, B., Mannle, T. E., Kivlahan, D. R., Paddock, S. M., ... Pincus, H. A. (2010). Transforming mental healthcare in the Veterans Health Administration: A model for measuring performance to improve access, quality, and outcomes. *Journal for Healthcare Quality, 32*(6), 33–43. doi:10.1111/j.1945-1474.2010.00109.x

Wayland, L., Holt, L., Sewell, S., Bird, J., & Edelman, L. (2010). Reducing the patient fall rate in a rural health system. *Journal for Healthcare Quality, 32*(2), 9–15. doi:10.1111 /j .1945-1474.2009.00068.x

Weiner, M., Callahan, C. M., Tierney, W. M., Overhage, J. M., Mamlin, B., Dexter, P. R., & McDonald, C. J. (2003). Using information technology to improve health care of older adults. *Annals of Internal Medicine, 139,* 430–436.

White, S. V. (2003). Second Annual Summit on Patient Safety and Information Technology. *Journal for Healthcare Quality, 25*(6), 38–39, 45. doi:10.1111/j.1945-1474.2003.tb01100.x

Wojtys, E. M., Schley, L., Overgaard, K. A., & Agbabian, J. (2009). Applying Lean techniques to improve the patient scheduling process. *Journal for Healthcare Quality, 31*(3), 10–16. doi:10.1111/j.1945-1474.2009.00025.x

Wolff, J. L., Roter, D. L., Given, B., & Gitlin, L. N. (2009). Optimizing patient and family involvement in geriatric home care. *Journal for Healthcare Quality, 31*(2), 24–33. doi:10.1111/j.1945-1474.2009.00016.x

Wright, K. B. (2011). A communication competence approach to healthcare worker conflict, job stress, job burnout, and job satisfaction. *Journal for Healthcare Quality, 33*(2), 7–14. doi:10.1111/j.1945-1474.2010.00094.x

Young, T., Brailsford, S., Connell, C., Davies, R., Harper, P., & Klein, J. H. (2004). Using industrial processes to improve patient care. *British Medical Journal, 328,* 162–164. doi:10.1136/bmj.328.7432.162

Zaratkiewicz, S., Whitney, J. D., Lowe, J. R., Taylor, S., O'Donnell, F., & Minton-Foltz, P. (2010). Development and implementation of a hospital-acquired pressure ulcer incidence tracking system and algorithm. *Journal for Healthcare Quality, 32,* 44–51. doi:10.1111/j.1945-1474.2010.00076.x

Online Resources

Accreditation Agencies

Accreditation Association for Ambulatory Health Care (AAAHC)
www.aaahc.org

Accreditation Commission for Health Care (ACHC)
www.achc.org

American Board for Certification in Orthotics, Prosthetics & Pedorthics
www.abcop.org/Pages/default.aspx

American College of Radiology (ACR) Accreditation
www.acr.org/accreditation.aspx

American Osteopathic Association (AOA) Healthcare Facilities Accreditation Program (HFAP)
www.hfap.org

American Society of Health-System Pharmacists (ASHP)
www.ashp.org/menu/Accreditation.aspx

CARF International
www.carf.org/home

College of American Pathologists (CAP) Accreditation and Laboratory Improvement
www.cap.org/apps/cap.portal?_nfpb=true&_pageLabel=accreditation

Community Health Accreditation Program
www.chapinc.org/Accreditation

Det Norske Veritas (DNV) National Integrated Accreditation for Healthcare Organizations (NIAHO)
http://dnvaccreditation.com/pr/dnv/badge-of-excellence.aspx

Healthcare Quality Association on Accreditation (HQAA)
www.achc.org

The Joint Commission
www.jointcommission.org

National Committee for Quality Assurance (NCQA)
www.ncqa.org

URAC
www.urac.org

Patient Engagement

Agency for Healthcare Research and Quality (AHRQ): Talking Quality
www.talkingquality.ahrq.gov/content/about/default.aspx

AHRQ Communication and Patient-Centered Care Toolkits
www.ahrq.gov/qual/pips/issues.htm

AHRQ Consumers and Patients
www.ahrq.gov/consumer/index.html

Americans for Quality Health Care Quality Tool Box: Consumer Engagement
www.nationalpartnership.org/site/PageServer?pagename=qcn_ToolBox_ConsumerEngagement

Partnership for Patients
www.healthcare.gov/compare/partnership-for-patients/index.htm

Patient-Centered Outcomes Research Institute
www.pcori.org

Quality Awards and Designations

AHCA/NCAL National Quality Award Program
www.ahcancal.org/quality_improvement/quality_award/pages/default.aspx

American Association of Critical-Care Nurses Beacon Award for Excellence
www.aacn.org/wd/beaconapps/content/mainpage.pcms?menu=beaconapps

ANCC Magnet Recognition Program
www.nursecredentialing.org/Magnet.aspx

Baldrige Performance Excellence Program (National Institute of Standards and Technology)
www.nist.gov/baldrige/

Department of Veterans Affairs Robert W. Carey Performance Excellence Award
www.va.gov/OP3/docs/Carey/Robert_W_Carey_Performance_Excellence_Award.asp

National Quality Forum and Joint Commission John M. Eisenberg Patient Safety and Quality Awards
www.jointcommission.org/topics/eisenberg_award.aspx

National Association for Healthcare Quality Awards
www.nahq.org/membership/leadership/prorecognition.html

Union of Japanese Scientists and Engineers Deming Prize
www.juse.or.jp/e

University of Utah Shingo Prize for Operational Excellence
www.shingoprize.org/model-guidelines.html

State, Local, and Regional Baldrige-Based Award Programs
www.nist.gov/baldrige/community/state_local.cfm

Index

W

Z